AQA Art & Design

AS A2

Student Handbook

Exclusively endorsed by AQA

Mike Ager
Roger Curtis
Stuart Helm
Series editor
Peter Dryland

Nelson Thornes

Published in 2008 by:
Nelson Thornes Ltd
Delta Place
27 Bath Road
CHELTENHAM
GL53 7TH
United Kingdom

08 09 10 11 12 / 10 9 8 7 6 5 4 3 2 1

A catalogue record for this book is available from the British Library

ISBN 978 0 7487 9912 1

Cover photograph/illustration: Alamy/Blend Images
Page make-up by Hart McLeod, Cambridge

Printed in Great Britain by Scotprint

The authors and publisher are grateful to the following for permission to reproduce photographs and other copyright material in this book:

p28: Fig. 1.36; p51: Fig. 1.65; p29: Fig. 1.37 Elliot Thoburn for The Telegraph's Seven Magazine; p30: Fig. 1.38 Ian Mckeever, Assembly Painting (FQ), 2006–2007 Acrylic and oil on linen 190 x 270cm ACG Ref P-2007-21 Illustrated p.15; p31: Fig. 1.39 Une Baignade a Asnieres: Bathers at Asnieres, 1884 (oil on canvas) by Seurat, Georges Pierre (1859–91) National Gallery, London, UK/ The Bridgeman Art Library; p33: Fig. 1.40 National Gallery; p33: Fig. 1.41 Monet La Grenouillere: La Grenouillere, 1869 (oil on canvas) by Monet, Claude (1840–1926) Metropolitan Museum of Art, New York, USA/ The Bridgeman Art Library; p34: Fig. 1.43 Nick Rose; p36: Fig. 1.45 The Lovers, 1928 (oil on canvas), Magritte, René (1898-1967) / Richard S. Zeisler Collection, New York, USA, © DACS / / The Bridgeman Art Library; p41: Fig. 5.1 The Fitzwilliam Museum, Cambridge; p42: Fig. 1.53 Gerhard Richter Wolken / Clouds (269) 1970 Oil on canvas 170 x 170 cm; p43: Fig. 1.55 Philadelphia Museum of Art: Gift of the Friends of Philadelphia Museum of Art in celebration of their twentieth anniversary, 1985; p45: Fig. 1.57 Manchester Art Gallery; p49: Fig. 1.63 Photo: Harry Shunk ©1970 Christo and Jeanne-Claude; p50: Fig. 1.64 Corbis Sygma/ Annebicque Bernard; p68: Fig. 2.8 View along an

Alpine Valley, possibly the Val d'Aosta (w/c) by Turner, Joseph Mallord William (1775–1851) Private Collection/ Photo © Christie's Images/ The Bridgeman Art Library; p76: Fig. 2.19 The Henry Moore Foundation Sculpture Settings by the Sea 1950 (HMF 2621); p116: Fig. 3.10; p119: Fig. 3.13; p121: Fig. 3.15 © Iain Stewart; p125: Fig. 3.19 (bottom) and p131: Fig. 3.29 "ECHO" – 2005, 64 x 66 inches, oil on canvas, Courtesy Allan Stone Gallery, NYC; p122: Fig. 3.16 Reflection (Self Portrait), 1985 by Freud, Lucian (b.1922) Private Collection/ The Bridgeman Art Library; p129: Fig. 3.26 Schoppleinstudio.com, Source: Courtesy of the Voulkos & Co. Catalogue Project www.voulkos.com; p130: Fig. 3.27 Audrey Walker; p153: Fig. 4.10 Extract from Hackney Flowers series by Stephen Gill; p154: Fig. 4.11 Howard Davis / Artifice Images; p155: Fig. 4.14 Artifice, Inc. / Artifice Images; p168: Fig. 4.35 Artifice, Inc. / Artifice Images; p174: Fig. 4.41 Tate Gallery; p175: Fig. 4.42 Thérèse Oulton c/o Marlborough Fine Art (London) Ltd; p176: Fig. 4.43 Flare-Up, 1992 (oil on canvas) by Oulton, Therese (b.1953), © Leeds Museums and Galleries (City Art Gallery) U.K./ The Bridgeman Art Library.

Contents

AQA introduction

Nelson Thornes and AQA

Nelson Thornes has worked in collaboration with AQA to ensure that this book offers you the best support for your A Level course and helps you to prepare for your exams. The partnership means that you can be confident that the range of learning, teaching and assessment practice materials has been checked by the senior examining team at AQA before formal approval, and is closely matched to the requirements of your specification.

Blended learning

Printed and electronic resources are blended: this means that links between chapters and case studies between the book and the electronic resources help you to work in the way that best suits you, and enable extra support to be provided online. Whilst the book provides you with a number of case studies, the online resources offer even more and in different media types.

Electronic resources are available in a simple-to-use online platform called Nelson Thornes learning space. If your school or college has a licence to use the service, you will be given a password through which you can access the materials through any internet connection.

Icons in this book indicate where there is material online related to that topic. The following icons are used:

Learning activity

All case studies in this book link to further online case studies, which will demonstrate similar assessment objectives across other endorsement areas, often exploring different themes and using different media.

When you see an icon, go to Nelson Thornes learning space at www.nelsonthornes.com/aqagce, enter your access details and select your course. The materials are arranged in the same order as the chapters in the book, so you can easily find the resources you need.

How to use this book

This book covers the specification for your course and is arranged in a sequence approved by AQA.

The book content is divided into chapters that match the AQA A Level Art & Design Specification. Each chapter concentrates on one of the four assessment objectives to help your progress through your AS (Unit 1 and Unit 2) and A2 (Unit 3 and Unit 4) Examinations.

The features in this book include:

Learning objectives

At the beginning of each chapter you will find a list of learning objectives that contain targets linked to the requirements of the specification.

Case study

Examples of work from actual A Level students and professional artists from all of the six endorsements, which demonstrate and contextualise the assessment objectives.

Key terms

Terms that you will need to be able to define and understand.

Links

Directs you to other parts of the book and highlights links between the assessment objectives. Suggested websites and publications are also included for further reading.

■ Remember

Provides you with valuable hints, tips and reminders.

■ Did you know?

Provides you with added bits of information.

AQA Examiner's tip

Tips from AQA Examiners, which will help you with your work across the four units.

Having read this chapter you should now be able to:

A bulleted list at the end of each chapter summarising the content in an easy-to-follow way.

■ Web links in the book

Because Nelson Thornes is not responsible for third party content online, there may be some changes to this material that are beyond our control. In order for us to ensure that the links referred to in the book are as up-to-date and stable as possible, the websites provided are usually homepages with supporting instructions on how to reach the relevant pages if necessary.

Please let us know at **webadmin@nelsonthornes.com** if you find a link that doesn't work and we will do our best to correct this at reprint, or to list an alternative site.

Introduction to the AQA Art & Design Student Handbook

About this book

This book has been compiled so that you have a better understanding of the revised AQA Art & Design A Level and are able to improve your chances of success. It begins with some thoughts about the value of undertaking a course in art and design and then explores the diverse nature of practice. There are many examples of different types of work, which have been linked to assessment criteria. It is important to remember that these are only examples. You will be expected to develop your own response and approach to your chosen area of study.

Why choose Art & Design?

An education in art and design should lead to a better understanding of the visual world and provide opportunities for you to develop your own visual language and the capacity to make informed, critical judgements. As visual communication is increasingly important this should give you the ability to express yourself effectively and help you to understand how ideas and information are communicated. You should become more confident when making aesthetic judgements and develop awareness of the different roles of artists, designers and craftspeople and photographers. In addition, you should gain valuable insights into your own and other cultures, and the contribution of the creative industries to society. You should also become aware of the importance of different audiences and consumers.

You may decide to go on to study art and design in further and higher education. An A Level course should help to provide you with a sound grounding of knowledge, skills and understanding as a foundation for further study. Furthermore, you should be able to develop the capacity to work independently.

Successful practice

Successful practice requires time and commitment but it can be highly rewarding. It is hoped that you will develop not only an interest in art, craft and design but enjoy producing your own work. You will need to develop a confident approach to your chosen area of study, whether it is in the field of Fine Art, Graphic Communication, Textile Design, Three-Dimensional Design, Photography, video or film.

An important aspect of practice in art and design is the need to develop effective skills in handling materials and media and an appreciation of different techniques and processes. The more that you have opportunities to develop your skills, the more effective you will become in communicating your ideas. Practice in art and design is based on a long history of skills and developing technologies, so you can learn much from the past experience of others.

Confidence with drawing is central to many art and design activities and this can only be improved through practise. You should have opportunities to make drawings on different scales, using a variety of media and approaches. These might range from small scale, closely observed studies, to much larger, expressive drawings. Keeping well-organised sketchbooks and workbooks can be really useful when gathering information and developing your ideas.

Writing

The A Level requires extended writing in one of the units in the second year but many students find it helpful to keep notes and add annotations to their work, throughout the course. These written materials can provide useful insights into your ideas and the reasons that you have made various choices. However, avoid filling every available space on mounted sheets or sketchbooks with writing, for the sake of it. Always consider whether the writing adds to the understanding of the work and provides genuine insights, rather than simply replicating what is already clear visually. Also, take care with the appearance, legibility, spelling, grammar and punctuation of your written work. Clumsy, misspelled writing and poor quality labelling can so easily let you down.

Using technology

During your A Level course you may have opportunities to use new technologies. Digital cameras are now widely used for recording by the majority of art and design students, as they provide a quick, easily accessible, means of recording. Many students also make extensive use of computers in their work. Accessing the Internet is useful for research. Computers are also widely used

for developing ideas and for producing finished work. Textile Design students often use computer software to develop repeating patterns and explore different colour ways. Graphic Communication students are able to quickly and easily access a wide range of fonts and explore the relationship of images and text. Three-Dimensional Design students often find it helpful to create virtual environments in which to site their work. Photography students often use computer software to enhance their digital images.

It is important to remember that there is a downside to the use of computers. Some material on the Internet is inappropriate, and occasionally illegal, so it is important to seek advice and guidance from your teachers and lecturers if you are unsure.

■ Projects

Throughout this book you will see references made to Projects. In the new A Level a Project is defined as a collection of work produced in response to an idea, issue or theme. In constructing a Project you should be able to demonstrate the ability to research and investigate your chosen starting point in some depth. This might be through a series of drawings, colour studies or photographs. Alternatively, you might explore the nature of different materials and techniques. Collections of images by other artists, designers or craftspeople might also form part of your research.

The ability to develop ideas is also an important aspect of Project work. You will need to show that you are able to sort through the material you have collected, with a critical eye, and consider a range of possible outcomes. These developments might take a variety of forms such as a collection of images, maquettes or models, representing different responses to the same theme, an exploration of different compositional arrangements or images that have been cropped or selectively enlarged.

Some aspect of your Project should relate to contextual sources in some way. This might include material that refers to the work of other artists, designers, craftspeople or photographers, who have explored a similar theme. It might also refer to some aspect of architecture or to work from a particular culture. A key consideration is that that you should provide evidence of learning from looking at the work of others. This could be demonstrated by making a similar response to an idea or by using a similar technique or approach. Reference might be made to some aspect of composition or the use of colour, shape, texture or form. The way that you display work might help to make connections with the work of others. This can be achieved visually by, for example, placing one image alongside another. Alternatively, you might choose to include written materials such as annotations which could highlight what has been learnt and how you have used your observations to inform your work.

■ The A Level Examination

The nature of the course of study you undertake will be different in different schools and colleges depending on the expertise of staff and available resources and facilities. Both AS and A2 (the second year) have a coursework unit and an externally set assignment. All units are of equal value.

The Portfolio Unit

This is the coursework unit at AS Level. The contents should be discussed with your teacher or lecturer. The Portfolio should reflect the nature of the course you have undertaken and should be carefully selected, organised and presented. It is not necessary or desirable to include everything you have produced. The Portfolio refers to a collection of two- or three-dimensional work which is likely to be produced mainly in the first part of the course but can be added to throughout the AS year. It can include sketchbooks, workbooks and journals as well as other preparatory work and final outcomes.

The contents of the Portfolio will vary from student to student but should reflect your particular interests and achievements. A Fine Art student might simply decide to include a single extended, in-depth Project, based on a theme such as Interiors or Global Warming. A student undertaking a Graphic Communication

course might wish to include three shorter Projects based on packaging, a corporate image and illustration. A Photography student might submit a workbook with examples of different processes, contact prints and information about well established photographers, alongside Projects based on documentary photography and portraiture.

During your course you might carry out a number of short tasks aimed at learning particular techniques, developing, for example, an understanding of different approaches to constructed textiles or different approaches to printmaking. Alternatively, you might have produced a number of life drawings. This type of work can also be included under the heading 'additional work'.

The AS Externally Set Assignment

On or near to 1st February you will receive an examination paper from AQA. This will include a number of broad-based starting points from which you will be expected to select one. These starting points should enable you to draw on the experiences you have had in the first part of the course. You should be able to make reference to artists with which you are already familiar. After a period of initial research of about two

to four weeks, you will have five hours of supervised, unaided time, when you will be expected to develop your ideas. The work you produce is up to you but it can take a variety of forms, such as a working drawing, a maquette, a model, a textile sample, work developed on a computer or in the darkroom, or a collection of design ideas. Following this you will have until the following May to complete your assignment, which is marked as a whole. There are no separate marks allocated to the five hour task.

■ The Personal Investigation

The Personal Investigation is the A2 coursework component. It includes the requirement that you should link a practical project with written material of 1000–3000 words. In order that you make a success of this unit you need to pay sufficient attention to both aspects of your work. A variety of approaches are acceptable but you should seek advice and guidance from your school or college staff.

The written element can be in the form of a written reflection on your practical project. This should provide insights into the main influences on your work, the development of the work and your reasons for making various choices. The work might include reports on gallery visits and critical analysis of your own or others' work.

Alternatively, the written element can be in the form of an extended, illustrated essay, based on an investigation into a particular theme, or some aspect of the work of an artist, designer, or craftsperson, an art, craft or design movement or culture. This should be linked in some way to your practical Project. It is important that when you select a topic for your study it should be small scale and achievable and give you an opportunity to develop a personal response. 'An Assessment of Six Contrasting Portraits by Picasso' would be fine, but 'The History of Fashion in the Twentieth Century' would be too challenging. If possible you should have reasonable access to original work in galleries or museums.

Whichever approach you adopt, you should include a bibliography, a list of any Internet sites you have used and any galleries or museums you have visited.

Written aspects of your work may take any appropriate form, such as a booklet, an illustrated essay, or a series of written statements placed alongside practical work. However, you need to ensure that you communicate clearly and in an appropriate form. The 1000–3000 word requirement relates to continuous prose. Annotations are not sufficient.

The A2 Externally Set Assignment

In this assignment you will have eight possible starting points from which you will be expected to select one. In this paper a number of artists, designers or craftspeople are mentioned in order to provide you with particular reference points for your research. However, these are included as examples and you may wish to identify other appropriate sources.

You will be given the examination papers in early February and your work should culminate in a period of supervised time of 15 hours in the following May, when you will be expected to complete finished work. All the work produced for this assignment will be marked together so you will need to provide evidence of your ability to research and develop ideas, making links with contextual work, and bringing your ideas to a successful conclusion.

Submitting work for assessment

It is essential that care is taken to select, organise and present work in a thoughtful manner ready for assessment. Some work might be mounted, others simply trimmed. Check that sketchbooks and workbooks are clearly labelled to avoid any confusion over which work relates to which Project. If you present your work effectively it should be easy to identify the original starting point and how your ideas have been researched and developed. The links with contextual materials should also be made clear. Aim to create a coherent journey from the original staring point to the final outcome.

Your questions answered

What do I need to produce for an Art & Design A Level?

There are two coursework units, a Portfolio unit at AS, and a Personal Investigation at A2. There are also 2 units set by AQA, an Externally Set Assignment at AS and a second Externally Set Assignment at A2.

Who is responsible for setting starting points for my work?

The emphasis in the A Level course should be on the development of individual work and a personal response. You might respond to an idea, issue or theme you have identified or you may respond to a starting point, or design brief set by your teachers or lecturers or AQA.

What should the Portfolio contain?

The Portfolio is effectively a collection of two-and/or three-dimensional work which reflects the nature of the AS course you have undertaken. There should be opportunities to experiment with media, develop skills, learn new techniques and explore a range of critical and historical materials. You should show evidence of your ability to research and develop ideas.

Are there any limitations to the contents of the Portfolio?

Portfolios must include at least *one project*. This should be a collection of work based on an idea, issue or theme which has a strong emphasis on the development of ideas. You may submit a single extended, in-depth project or several projects, but this will depend on the nature of the course you have undertaken. You can also submit *additional work* such as a collection of life drawings, experiments with different materials or work resulting from a gallery visit or artist's residency. You might include wide-ranging workbooks or sketchbooks packed with different materials, demonstrating the range of your interests or, perhaps, something more focused. Sketchbooks are not necessarily essential as a series of images on mounted sheets or a collection of drawings or colour studies can be equally effective.

Apart from containing at least one project are there limitations on the contents of the Portfolio?

There are no limitations on the size or contents but you should select, organise and present your work carefully in order to make connections between different elements, such as aspects of your own work and that of others. You should also, whenever possible, demonstrate how your work and ideas have developed.

Do I have to include critical/contextual work?

You are expected to produce work which is *informed by contextual and other sources*. Evidence can be included wholly in a visual form but it can also include written and oral evidence, e.g. through video and audio tapes. Critical/contextual work is required in all four units.

What is an Externally Set Assignment?

There are two externally set assignments, one in AS and a second in A2. Both units commence with the distribution of question papers on the 1st February and marks should be sent to AQA and the moderator to arrive by 31st May.

What is the nature of Unit 2 the AS Externally Set Assignment?

- This has five broad-based questions or starting points. Specific contextual references are not included but the questions should allow you to make reference to artists, designers, craftspeople and photographers with whom you are already familiar.
- After an initial period set aside for researching and investigating your chosen starting point, you will undertake five hours of supervised time. During this time you will need to produce work which demonstrates how you intend to develop your ideas. This may take any appropriate form such as a working drawing, a maquette, a colour study, or a sheet of design ideas.
- Following the five hours of supervised time you can either produce more work of a developmental nature or bring your work to a final realisation(s).

What is the nature of the Unit 4 A2 Externally Set Assignment?

This is similar to Unit 2. The main differences are that you will have eight questions which include the names of specific artists and the supervised time of 15 hours comes at the end of the examination period. Question papers will be issued on the 1st February and all work should be completed and marked by the end of May of the second year. All marks should be sent to AQA and the moderator to arrive by 31st May.

How will the Externally Set Assignments be supervised?

- The AS five hour and A2 15 hour supervised times should be treated in the same way as other timed examinations. You should work independently, with an invigilator present, in a quiet working environment.

- Other requirements will be in place for the rest of the examination period between February and May. Following the distribution of question papers, you may discuss the selection of starting point with your teacher or lecturer. You will then work independently producing a personal response. Teachers/lecturers will monitor and discuss the progress of the work with you. This is important for a number of reasons. It will ensure that the work you submit is your own. It should help you to avoid using contextual materials, particularly from the Internet, that might be considered unsuitable, and it should help you to avoid working with dangerous materials or working in unsafe ways.
- It is important to note that all work produced for an Externally Set Assignment is *marked as a whole*. There are no separate marks allocated for the work produced in the five or 15 hours of Supervised Time.

What is required for Unit 3 – the Personal Investigation?

You will be expected to produce and link both written and visual materials in this unit. Written materials should be 1000–3000 words in length. They should be in the form of extended writing rather that in note form. This means that a series of annotations in a sketchbook will not be appropriate. You will need to ensure that:

- text is legible and that spelling, punctuation and grammar are accurate so that meaning is clear;
- you use a form and style of writing appropriate to complex subject matter;
- you organise information clearly and coherently, using specialist vocabulary when appropriate.

The written component should be taken seriously. You should use specialist language related to art and design whenever possible and make sure that your work is carefully checked and can be readily understood.

Can I write a formal personal study?

You may decide to write an in-depth illustrated essay based on some aspect of the work of artists, designers, craftspeople or photographers. This can be in book form but might be presented in a less conventional way such as a collection of boxes, a folding screen or as part of an interesting sculptural form. It is important to remember that your essay needs to be linked to an aspect of your practical work in some way.

Can I approach written work in a different way?

As an alternative to a long essay you may decide to focus on your own work. You could keep a journal, write a commentary, or include written materials within a practical project. This written material should aim to shed light on your ideas, influences on the development of your ideas and the reasons you have made various decisions. You may also wish to make reference to gallery or studio visits. If for any reason your written work is difficult to read, it is a good idea to provide a word processed copy for examiners.

Are other approaches acceptable?

You might wish to adopt a mixture of the two approaches outlined above, including written material that focuses on your own practice alongside a more formal study.

Are there other requirements for the Personal Investigation?

You should, whenever possible, see work at first hand although this might not always be possible such as when looking at site-specific work of artists such as Christo and Richard Long. You should also list the sources used to inform your work, such as galleries visited, a bibliography and list of Internet sites visited.

Do I need to include written materials with every project or unit?

Written work is only compulsory in Unit 3, the Personal Investigation. Other units can be wholly practical but if written materials are included, make sure they add to the understanding of the practical work. Avoid adding notes and annotations as a form of 'wallpaper' simply replicating what has already been made clear visually. Remember that unnecessary labelling can detract from visual material. Heavy handed titles made with a marker pen can ruin a carefully organised and otherwise well presented mounted sheet.

Who will mark my work?

All work will be marked initially by teachers and lecturers in centres. Moderators will then visit centres to check that the marks are in line with national standards.

1 Developing ideas

Fig. 1.1 *Mixed-media study*

Ideas rarely appear from nowhere and every kind of idea needs working at. Ideas can develop as you investigate contextual sources, experiment with **media**, materials and **techniques**, when you review and refine your ideas, record your observations and insights, and realise your intentions.

The investigation of contextual sources is an important element in the development process. It can open your eyes to possibilities and help to shape your own work. Acquiring the knowledge to demonstrate analytical and critical skills should help you to understand in more depth the process of investigation and the development of ideas.

In this chapter you will learn how to:

■ develop ideas through sustained and focused investigations

■ develop ideas informed by contextual and other sources

■ demonstrate analytical and critical understanding.

■ **Key terms**

Media: plural of 'medium'; the materials of art and design activity, e.g. pencil, crayon, chalk, charcoal, clay, plaster, wire, thread.

Techniques: ways in which materials and media can be manipulated to create different visual effects.

Fig. 1.2 *Location study in watercolour and chalk*

Fig. 1.3 *Photograph on location*

Fig. 1.4 *Ideas in graphics*

Key terms

Fieldwork: gallery or museum visits, site visits, work done on location.

Starting point: an object, theme, issue or brief.

Source material: objects, artefacts or images that you will investigate and develop your ideas from.

Design brief: a defined focus for a topic that has specific requirements, for example in Graphic Communication.

Remember

Discuss your ideas and intentions with your art teacher.

Examiner's tip

When planning fieldwork:

■ plan your work and manage your time effectively

■ consider investigating local resources.

Did you know?

If you plan to use an industrial location such as a factory or a scrapyard for your fieldwork:

■ you may need permission in advance

■ it may be necessary to consider whether it is a safe working environment.

If planning to make notes and take photos in shopping malls and supermarkets, or of shop window displays, you may need permission.

Remember

Do you need to consider the cost of travel and entrance fees?

■ Approaches to the development of ideas

Selecting a starting point

Starting points and ideas can originate from your personal investigations and experiences, from **fieldwork** that might include site visits, location work and gallery study, from something you have seen or from an event or an issue. Usually you will develop ideas in response to a starting point, a theme or brief given to you by your art teacher or provided by an externally set assignment.

When selecting a **starting point**, consider what you are most interested in and the opportunities that presents. Will the starting point you have chosen enable you to make the best use of your abilities, to develop your strengths and help you to perform to the best of your ability? Also, consider the availability of source material and access to it. Can you obtain enough **source material** that is appropriate? Will it supply you with the information you need to develop your ideas? Do you have the resources, materials and equipment as well as the knowledge, skill and understanding to work from a particular starting point?

Sometimes you will be able to instantly identify an appropriate and inspiring starting point. Perhaps it is something that immediately arouses your interest, or something you are already interested in. Perhaps it looks like the sort of starting point that you could become interested in if you could get exciting source material and develop an interesting angle to your investigation. To begin, you might wish to explore more than one starting point or investigate more than one initial idea.

Getting started

Once you have selected your starting point, identify its main features. A **design brief** usually has specific requirements. You might use a technique such as word storming or 'mind mapping', or make use of a thesaurus to help expand the question so that you can generate initial ideas. Simple techniques like these can help you to think your way around the problem and will point you towards appropriate source material. Once you have established what material you think you will need you can begin to plan how you will set about obtaining it.

Resourcing ideas

Source material can take many forms depending on the nature of the starting point. Whatever source material you collect, you need to be selective and the material should be relevant to what you are aiming to do. Resourcing ideas and identifying the material to work from could involve fieldwork in the natural or built environment, visits to museums or galleries or exploring resources such as libraries, books, exhibition catalogues, magazines, newspapers and the internet. You might also have the opportunity to visit or work with practising artists, craftspeople and designers in their studios or in workshops organised by your school or college.

In case study 2 (p12), Michael resourced his work from material he obtained from books, the internet and from fieldwork at a museum.

Case study 1

Resourcing ideas in Fine Art

Dasal is an A Level student whose Unit 3 was resourced from fieldwork in which he took a series of photographs and made, on site, quick A5- and A6-size studies of dramatic cloud formations against a spectacular sunset.

Fig. 1.5 *A dramatic cloud and sunset*

Fig. 1.6 *Location study in watercolour and chalk*

Fig. 1.7 *Location study in pen, fineliner, Conté crayon, mud*

Fig. 1.8 *Location study*

Fig. 1.9 *Location study in Conté crayon and watercolour*

The location studies used a range of media and techniques that included watercolour and mixed media such as pen, fineliner, Conté crayon and mud found on site. He had to work quickly as the light changed rapidly over two evenings' work, but the idea of 'time' became an important aspect of his work as it developed.

Dasal's photos and studies made on location were used to develop his ideas and his preparatory work in the studio. The time spent in the field, in direct contact with his source material, gave his work the benefit of an intense, vivid experience from which to develop his ideas.

Gathering or collecting source material can involve a number of research techniques such as:

■ taking a sketchbook and camera into the environment
■ collecting objects or specimens
■ collecting and investigating images.

Collecting resources should be a focused activity. Avoid gathering resources in an aimless manner, collecting inappropriate or irrelevant material for the sake of it. Remember that you are gathering visual information that will supply you with the material you need to develop your ideas. Be aware of your strengths and weaknesses and consider carefully the potential for development in the resources you collect.

 Case study 2

Resourcing ideas in Three-Dimensional Design

Michael's AS project in Three-Dimensional Design is a response to a Unit 2 externally set assignment that prompted him to study ways in which communal spaces such as piazzas, playgrounds and shopping malls can be enhanced by sculptures, installations or landscaping. He began resourcing his ideas, obtaining photos of birds in flight, skeletons, ribs and spines, from books and the internet. He also visited a museum in Liverpool to get images of dinosaur bones. From this source material, Michael was able to make loose initial drawings and a series of more sustained analytical drawings that would inform the development of his ideas.

Fig. 1.10 *Study*

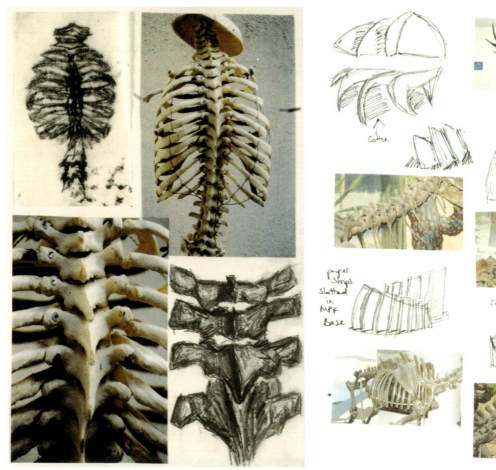

Fig. 1.11 *One of Michael's study sheets*

Fig. 1.12 *Thumbnail sketches and photos of bones*

Sources

You can gather source material in a variety of forms: drawings, **colour** notes, photos, reproductions and images, objects, surfaces and materials, depending upon the nature of your starting point. You can choose to make studies from direct observation of first-hand sources or from secondary sources. Aim for the best-quality source material that you can get.

The camera can be used as an effective recording and sketchbook tool. Although the quality of your camera can have a significant impact on the quality of your photos, reasonably good equipment handled properly should give good results. Occasionally, useful images can be made using less sophisticated equipment such as a mobile phone, but whatever means are used, you should aim to make images that are clear and informative and that help you to develop your ideas.

Key terms

Colour: the colours of the spectrum: red, blue, yellow, green, orange, violet, etc.

Links

■ See Chapter 2 for ideas about selecting resources.

■ See Chapter 3 for ideas about recording observations.

Case study 3

Resourcing ideas in Graphic Communication

Nick is an AS student who has responded to a graphics brief requiring ideas for a logo design for a water supply company.

He did fieldwork at a local lake where he took a series of photographs in which he explored the movement and shapes of ripples.

Fig. 1.13 *Shapes in moving water*

Fig. 1.14 *One of a series of photos*

He took a large number of photographs from which he selected the most informative and best-quality images. This enabled him to make a series of small drawings that explored the shape, rhythm and movement of the water. His photographs and drawings provided him with the material from which he was able to explore and develop shapes, and these formed the basis for the development of his ideas.

Case study 4

An artist resourcing ideas in Photography

Reinhild Beuther studied the History of Art in Berlin, and Sculpture, Ceramics and Photography in Kiel before moving to the UK to study for an MA in Sculpture at the Royal College of Art in London. She has exhibited in Germany, the US and the UK. Reinhild is a founder member of ArtNucleus, set up as a focal point for artists working on multimedia projects. Her project, *Uta von Naumburg*, started when Reinhild visited Naumburg Cathedral where she was fascinated by a group of sculptures from the early Romanesque period. The sculptures portray figures of highly educated women who, in medieval times, often played a role in German politics.

■ Link

To view more of Reinhild's work and projects, see www.artnucleus.org

Fig. 1.15 *Naumburg Cathedral*

Fig. 1.16 *Uta*

Figure 1.16 is an example of one of the sculptures of Uta, a medieval queen, that Reinhild saw at Naumburg. She was also interested in the atmosphere and sense of history that she found in the cathedral. Her work was resourced by finding images in books, buying postcards and by research using the internet. She made a second visit to the cathedral to soak up the atmosphere and take her own photographs.

Link

See Chapter 2 for more ideas about exploring media, techniques and processes.

Starting to develop ideas

Ideas can begin to develop as soon as you start trying to locate appropriate source material. In case study 1, Dasal saw possibilities in a spectacular sky that he photographed, and made quick studies from, in a field next to his garden. This was not pre-planned. He experienced the event and seized the opportunity. In case study 3, Nick organised a short field trip to a local lake to take his photographs of water, and in case study 2, Michael identified the kind of source material that he wanted and took himself off to the Liverpool Museum in search of bones and skeletons.

But fieldwork is not the only way of getting source material and starting to develop an idea. If you were planning to study natural objects such as pine cones as the basis of a textile design, the source material might be near to hand, at home or in the art room. In case study 10, Stuart began his study of the figure by investigating the work of other artists and, in his Three-Dimensional Design project, Michael began by looking at examples of structures in public places. No matter how you obtain your source material, whether by fieldwork, or finding objects, or browsing books or the internet for images or **contextual material**, as soon as you have identified what you need and set about obtaining it, you will have the beginnings of an idea or several ideas.

Whether taking photographs, drawing and painting or collecting material and images, gathering source material also involves selection. You will naturally choose what you consider to be the best, most promising, most interesting images or objects. From this material you will continue to select so that you begin to focus your ideas, looking for the best **content**, angle, eye-level and viewpoint, studying close to and further away and cropping images. These kinds of choices will be made as you begin to think in a visual, creative way in response to the source material you have gathered and as you develop your ideas through exploring and analysing it and experimenting with media and processes.

Case study 5

Developing ideas in Fine Art

Dasal explored his source material using a range of media and processes. His ideas developed gradually as he made a sequence of studies ranging from quick initial studies, that he made in order to get a feel for what the source material had to offer, to sustained analytical studies and those that enabled him to investigate and explore ways in which he could handle media and exploit scale to express his ideas.

This process was informed by contextual material that Dasal investigated as his work progressed. As his investigation advanced, he identified ideas which he wanted to develop, including:

- layers in the spectacular cloud formations and dramatic colour
- the notion of time and movement as the clouds and light quickly changed
- the way in which we look across the landscape towards the distant sky, gradually looking more and more upwards until we are looking directly up at the sky overhead
- the way in which we can 'read' the image as a sky and landscape, or as a landscape and the layers beneath the ground.

Fig. 1.17 *Sketchbook studies*

Fig. 1.18 *Studies in Conté crayon*

Key terms

Composition: the way in which each part of an image or form relates to each other and to the whole.

The black-and-white Conté study, Fig 1.19, developed the vertical **composition** on a larger scale, 120cm × 84cm, and focuses on the idea of looking across, up and overhead, a turning point in the development of Dasal's ideas.

Using acrylic, graphite and Conté, Dasal began to explore colour and paint handling to express and develop his ideas.

As the idea of ambiguity gradually became the focus of the work, it moved away from its original starting point as a sunset over a darkened landscape. Dasal also explored scale and, influenced by some of his contextual material, he explored proportion so that the image finally became compressed in a long, narrow rectangle, 120cm × 60cm, Figure 1.21,that makes the spectator's eyes follow the journey towards the horizon then upwards until looking overhead.

Fig. 1.19 *Study in Conté crayon*

Fig. 1.20 *Charcoal study*

Fig. 1.21 *Working drawing*

Establishing a clear focus to the development of ideas

An important element in the process of developing ideas is the ability to establish a clear focus in your investigation and to sustain your line of thinking so that the work develops fluently. The work should reflect the 'journey' that you make in exploring source material, developing an angle or focus that will drive your investigation towards a strong, well-conceived idea. Your preparatory work should reflect the ways in which you have considered alternatives and the decisions that you have made. It should demonstrate your thinking as the project develops.

The beginnings of ideas can emerge even at the earliest stage of the work, whilst you are gathering and evaluating source material, investigating contextual sources or working your way through initial drawings, colour studies or photographs. A clear focus to your ideas and direction within your work should emerge and become established as you analyse your source material, recording your observations in sustained analytical studies and exploring media and processes. Sustained observation and analysis of your source material should reveal the characteristics and qualities that you will want to exploit.

As your preparatory work progresses, your ideas should develop as your intentions and the focus of the work become more clear. You may well change the focus of your idea and the direction of your preparatory work as your understanding of your source material and your response to it develops. In case study 5 we saw how Dasal's ideas developed and changed emphasis as his work became more abstract and expressive.

■ Link

See Chapter 2 for more ideas in experimenting with media, techniques and processes.

Case study 6

Developing ideas in Graphic Communication

In this example of developing ideas in graphics, Nick has made a sustained and focused investigation of the brief's requirements and the source material from which he explored and developed his ideas for a company logo design.

He investigated shapes in moving water, making line drawings from his own photographs, and also looked at ways that a number of artists have interpreted water in their paintings.

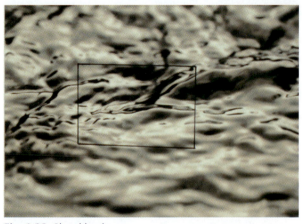

Fig. 1.22 *Sketchbook page*

Fig. 1.23 *Line drawings*

From his initial drawings, Nick developed a series of abstract shapes that reflect the qualities of water. He evaluated these and selected what he considered to be the most promising shapes to form the basis of his design ideas. Using electronic media and Adobe Photoshop, these were redrawn and manipulated in a logical development and sequence, gradually forming the image that would be the basis of the logo design.

Fig. 1.24 *Developing ideas*

He then investigated typography, exploring a wide range of fonts and experimenting with colour and tonal values.

SouthvaleWater   *Southvale Water*

Southvale Water   Southvale Water

Fig. 1.25 *Investigating typography*

Type and artwork were brought together through a sequence of studies that investigated and developed the relationship between type, image and space.

Fig. 1.26 *Type and image*

Fig. 1.27 *Final logo design on a business card*

Finally, Nick developed his ideas for the application of the logo design on the side of a delivery van. He explored the design problem of relating his logo design to the shape and space available on the vehicle and decided to incorporate it into his ideas for van livery. Nick explored the relationship between the logo, livery and space, giving careful consideration to the balance between these elements in developing and refining his ideas. Much thought and reflection went into the scale and weight of the logo and livery as well as the balance and weight of tonal values.

Fig. 1.28 *Developing ideas*

Fig. 1.29 *Final idea*

Investigations

In case study 6 Nick's work is a clear illustration of the interdependence and overlap of the assessment objectives. For example, assessment objective 2 (experimenting with media, materials, techniques and processes) and assessment objective 3 (recording your observations, experiences and insights) will inform and advance the development of your ideas.

Discoveries about your source material, the ways in which you have handled a medium or technique, or the ways that you have chosen a particular viewpoint and eye level, can trigger an angle that can drive your idea or expose other ways of approaching it. Sometimes an accidental discovery can encourage you to explore a new direction. Always be open to and alert to the unexpected.

It is important to sustain your investigation, to keep up the momentum and keep it moving across the project as a whole, ensuring that you address each of the assessment objectives. Not all studies will take the same amount of time. Loose, initial thumbnail sketches and drawings will take less time than more sustained, analytical studies where you are searching in more depth.

Your investigations and evidence of the development of your ideas can be presented in a number of ways. You might choose to produce all of your preparatory work on sheets which are later mounted, or in sketchbooks, workbooks or journals, or you might use a combination. Alternatively, you might work in an area of study or in a medium in which it is appropriate to present your work using digital or electronic means.

Composition and design in developing ideas

A key element in the process of developing ideas is producing compositions, **designs**, **maquettes**, **samples** or **contact prints**.

- In Fine Art this might involve a process of selection from source material and your studies by cropping or enlarging. You should explore the way that each shape or form relates to each other and to the whole composition, and how the image as a whole relates to the **framing edge**. Small **compositional roughs**, **design roughs** or **thumbnail sketches** are often used to explore and manipulate ideas, gradually refining the relationship between different elements.

- In Sculpture and Three-Dimensional Design, working drawings, maquettes or models help to clarify and define aspects of form, mass, volume and **space**.

- In Graphic Comunication, **thumbnail drawings** or diagrams can often help to explore and plan the ways in which the **design elements** of a page layout relate to the edge of a page, or the ways in which image, type and space can relate to each other. They can also be used to explore the development of a storyboard or **animated sequence**.

- In Photography, contact prints will help to identify the most promising images. Often they have a very important role in the development of ideas and in the process of evaluation and selection of images. **Thumbnails** or roughs can be used to reflect on and think through ideas or to analyse compositional problems. They might help in the consideration of how images will relate to each other and the best format for presentation. For example, the idea might progress towards the production of a sequence or series of images to be viewed as a whole, or a single image.

- In Textile Design, small loosely drawn roughs, samples or experiments with media, and studies exploring techniques, textures and **colourways** can help explore and develop ideas for a fabric print, a garment or wall hanging.

Link

See Chapter 2 for information about refining ideas.

💡 Case study 7

Developing ideas in Three-Dimensional Design

This case study illustrates a clear sense of a creative journey through the student's investigation and the development of his ideas. Michael's photographs have provided the source material for a line of enquiry to be established from his initial sketches and notes. Figure 1.30, a sample page from the student's sketchbook, shows, in the small studies, the beginnings of abstract form and the generation of ideas.

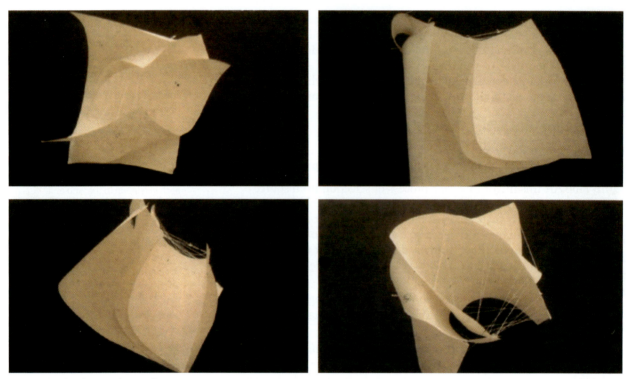

Fig. 1.30 *Developing abstract form*

Remember

A key element in developing ideas is producing compositions, designs, maquettes, samples or contact prints.

Key terms

Visuals: visualisations or 'mock-ups' using a photo-montage technique to show, for example, how an idea for a large sculpture or construction might look in a landscape, a built environment or public space.

His investigations lead to ideas in which he considered and documented a number of potential locations in Liverpool for his 3D construction, including the Albert Dock and several city squares. Contextual material is well integrated into the development process and it informs the development of ideas. As we see in Figure 1.31, sequences of 3D models, or maquettes, constructed using paper, show the student making a logical progression by manipulating his ideas in 3D.

In the final stages of the project, he used computer software to produce a series of visuals in which his projected construction is sited in various city-centre environments and locations. The visuals are a significant feature of the work as they give context to the development of Michael's ideas, and through them we gain an extra insight into his consideration and understanding of scale.

Figure 1.32 is the final study in a series of visuals that explore potential sites for the construction. Throughout the work, his decision making is transparent and easy to understand.

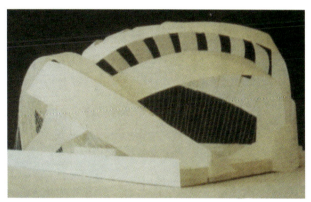

Fig. 1.31 *Maquettes*

Fig. 1.32 *Visual of the final idea*

Key terms

Electronic media: computer hardware, video and sound recording.

AQA Examiner's tip

If you use computer software, document the techniques and processes you have used.

Link

See Chapter 2 for more ideas about experimenting with media, techniques and processes.

Did you know?

In some areas of study, especially Photography and Graphic Communication, you might choose to present your work in the form of a digital sketchbook.

Electronic media

Electronic media and software are an invaluable resource for obtaining information and processing it, but they can also provide the means for manipulating and combining images, which can add much to the ways in which you can explore and develop ideas.

■ Drawings and images can be scanned. Images can be pulled together and layered, shapes can be developed and manipulated, alternative colourways can be explored.

■ Electronic media are also used extensively in graphics as a drawing tool, for combining images with type, for developing designs of page layouts and for developing design applications.

■ In Photography, processing digital images, using software such as Adobe Photoshop, provides opportunities for selecting, cropping, enlarging, combining and manipulating images, which add greatly to the possibilities for developing ideas.

■ In Textile Design too, software can be used to explore textures, surfaces, pattern, tone and colour in a way that offers exciting and profitable possibilities.

■ Computer software can be used, not only to manipulate the content of ideas and compositional alternatives, but also to explore, visualise and develop the ways in which, for example, a proposed large environmental sculpture, Three-Dimensional Design, installation or construction might be installed in the landscape or urban location (see case study 7).

In using computer software to develop your ideas, it is important to provide evidence of the development and the decisions you have made so that the process can be easily read and understood. Documenting this process needs patience and organisation to demonstrate the journey taken in the development of your ideas. You can do this by printing off the stages in the development of, for example, a logo design, demonstrating the developments and changes you make as your ideas advance and progress. You can also provide screengrabs (see case study 6) to document the techniques and processes you have used in manipulating your work.

💡 Case study 8

An artist developing ideas in Photography

The artist, Reinhild Beuther, explores the same theme repeatedly in her work, changing the emphasis slightly. Using Adobe Photoshop to manipulate images, she has produced work in which images of her own face are layered with the faces of famous people from history who she acknowledges and cherishes. Reinhild's work is an example of a practising artist who has established a focus to her work in which sustained investigation informs the development of her ideas.

In *Uta von Naumburg*, Reinhild developed her idea by layering her own image with numerous images of Uta, the medieval German queen.

Figure 1.34 shows the layering of an image of Reinhild's face with an image of Uta, taken from an early Romanesque sculpture.

Fig. 1.33 *Uta von Naumburg*

Fig. 1.34 *Layered image*

Using annotations in developing ideas

You are required to make a written response *only* in Unit 3, the personal investigation. However, **annotations** are sometimes used as a developmental tool to help establish or maintain the focus of investigations and ideas development. They can help to clarify, in your own mind, possible avenues of investigation or to identify, shape and plan the direction you are taking.

They can also make clear the decisions and connections made in the development process, where this would otherwise be unclear or open to misinterpretation.

Usually it is easy to follow the progress of a project by way of evidence of the journey that the work has made, especially when studies are clearly linked to each other and the development process is visually clear to read. Annotations are useful only when they give additional insights and add to the understanding of the work.

In Photography, whether using lens-based or light-based media, and in Graphic Communication, it is especially important to document the process of your work. This might include technical information such as:

- cameras and lenses used
- shutter speed, aperture, film speed
- darkroom techniques and printing papers used
- the use of computer software, masks or filters.

Fig. 1.35 *Documenting process*

■ Did you know?

Iain Stewart is a professional photographer whose ideas are a very personal response to remote landscapes and seascapes. His images explore light, colour and atmosphere.

Fig. 1.36 *Ideas in Photography: First Light,* © *Iain Stewart*

Fig. 1.37 *Ideas in Graphic Communication, Elliot Thoburn: illustration*

Investigation and developing ideas in the written element of Unit 3

In Unit 3, the personal investigation, you are required to produce a practical project and written material of 1,000–3,000 words that is linked to it. In both the practical and written work, you should develop ideas through a sustained and focused investigation.

■ Your written material might be a reflection on elements within your practical project in the unit, with an emphasis on the development of ideas. You might choose to include an evaluation of your practical work.

■ You might make a Personal Study that investigates an aspect of art, craft, or design practice that relates to your own practical work. You could, for example, investigate the work of an artist, designer or craftsperson that you are making reference to in developing your own work, or you could investigate work that shares a theme or issue, a medium, process or technique.

Fig. 1.38 *Ian McKeever, Assembly Painting (FQ), 2006–2007 Acrylic and oil on linen 190 x 270cm*

A written reflection on your practical work

You might choose to produce a written reflection on the nature of your practical work, the ways in which ideas have been developed and how contextual material has informed the development of your ideas. It might explore the ways in which experimentation with materials, processes and techniques has enabled you to develop and refine your ideas and might include an evaluation of your work.

Choosing an appropriate topic for a Personal Study

To be effective in your investigation and in developing ideas, you need to make sure that the topic you choose is appropriate so that it will connect successfully with your practical work.

It also needs a clear, well-defined focus or angle so that your work has a clear sense of direction. Your investigation should be carried out in some depth, so do not make the mistake of choosing a topic that is too large and too broad.

Like any investigation, the work needs to be planned and organised. A clear set of objectives or questions might help you to give the investigation a shape or framework. It would help to break up the information that you need into smaller, more manageable bites and it would give a good idea of the sequence in which you will gather material and information.

In considering your ideas for the topic, make sure that you will have access to appropriate contextual source materials so that you will be able to gather the information you need. Investigate the availability of contextual material that might be in galleries or museums, the availability of books, articles, exhibition catalogues and images, and look at the usefulness of the internet. Your initial investigations should identify what is available and what you have access to.

Investigating the topic

The investigation of your topic needs to be sustained. Information and contextual material needs to be identified, gathered and read or looked at, and you will need to make notes recording your observations and insights. You might choose to consider the ideas of other authors, specialists, historians and critics of art, craft and design. Analysing and evaluating contextual material in depth will enable you to develop your own ideas as you respond to the work you are studying, and these ideas should connect with and inform the development of ideas in your practical work.

Attention should be given to the clarity, coherence and accuracy of the written work and you should be able to demonstrate your understanding of **specialist language**. Avoid relying simply on descriptive writing in which ideas are not developed. Analysis is also important. Investigate not just the 'what' and describe it, but also investigate the 'how' and 'why'.

Acknowledge your sources using captions to illustrations and reproductions, recording the artist, title, date and any other relevant information that you might wish to include, such as the medium used, the work's dimensions, the gallery or owner. Record in a **bibliography** the details of any books, exhibition catalogues, periodicals, articles, websites, videos or DVDs used as research sources. It is good practice to list these details in standard form: author, title, publisher, year.

Key terms

Specialist language: the words that are used to define the formal elements of art, craft and design and additional terms that give more detail such as hue, tint, shade, tone, foreground, background, plane, positive and negative shape, translucence, opacity. Each subject area in art, craft and design also has terms that are specific to their media and processes.

Bibliography: a list which documents books, articles, websites, etc. used as sources. It is usually presented in standard form – author, title, publisher, year (if known).

Did you know?

The date a book is published is usually shown in small print on the reverse of the title page.

Fig. 1.39 *Georges Seurat,* Une Baignade, Asnières, *1883–84*

Remember

Contextual material can be gathered as the work progresses.

Did you know?

Sources can be selected for a range of aspects and purposes to inform the development of your work.

AQA Examiner's tip

■ Select contextual sources appropriate to your work.

■ Use them effectively to inform its development.

■ Do not just collect material to tick the box.

■ Using contextual materials to inform investigations

Sources that you select should be appropriate and relevant to your work. They might be chosen to investigate **subject** or content, colour and **tonal relationships**, the application of techniques and media, the use of space or composition. The selection of contextual materials is often an ongoing process, gathering and exploring material in the preparatory stages of a project. Also, it is possible to gather relevant images from outside your area of study. For example, it is not unusual for work in Graphic Communication, Photography or Textile Design to make connections with the work of fine artists. Researching and investigating contextual material, the work of other artists, designers and craftspeople, should genuinely inform the development of your ideas. In the development of a project you might investigate works that are relevant for the ways in which:

■ a subject or theme has been interpreted or responded to

■ a medium or technique has been manipulated and used

■ formal elements have been used

■ colour, tone, pattern and texture have been used

■ aspects of composition, **layout** or **design** have been manipulated.

The process and purpose of identifying and collecting contextual material is sometimes misunderstood. Students often obtain these sources only at the start of a unit or after initial recording from their source material. It is important to realise that gathering contextual material can take place more naturally as the work proceeds, to genuinely inform the development of your work.

💡 Case study 9

Using contextual material in Graphic Communication

Nick investigated the work of Monet and Seurat (see Figures 1.39, 1.40 and 1.41), in connection with his study of water. Initially both were accessed using books and the National Gallery website, but later he had the opportunity to study these and other relevant works at the gallery.

Looking at the work of these artists helped Nick to think in more depth about the ways he could respond to the photos he took of moving water and interpret graphically the movement and ripples.

Nick also investigated examples of existing logo designs for water companies (see Figure 1.42) which he analysed in detailed annotations, making references to the characteristics of shapes, the expression of the idea of water and its purity, and the handling of colour, typography, space and composition.

He also researched a number of designs for van livery that incorporated company logos (see Figure 1.43). Analysis and evaluation of these designs increased his awareness and understanding of the relationship between the design elements used, knowledge that he was able to use to inform his investigations in resolving problems and in refining his designs.

Fig. 1.40 *Monet,* Bathers at Grenouillere, *1869*

Fig. 1.41 *Monet,* La Grenouillere, *1869*

Fig. 1.42 *Other water company logos*

Fig. 1.43 *Other van livery designs*

What sort of contextual material?

Contextual material can take a variety of forms and can be obtained from various sources. You might research material from visits to galleries, museums, workshops or studios, and in the case of Graphic Communication you might need to look for live material. This might include packaging and label designs in retail outlets, exhibition or

Fig. 1.44 *Mike Finch of Winchcombe Pottery*

promotional Graphic Communication graphics applied to buildings or transport in the form of logo and livery designs, or the environment in the form of signs and signage systems.

Whatever your area of study, first-hand experience of contextual material has benefits. Direct observation and experience can be more immediate, more fresh and vivid than relying solely on found images and reproductions. However, investigating contextual material in books and on gallery websites, or browsing the websites of contemporary and past artists, illustrators and designers, can offer a breadth of experience, giving access to extensive resources and collections from which you can be selective.

You may be fortunate enough to have access to practising artists and their studios, craftspeople and their workshops, visits to your school by artists, workshops at school or in local galleries, or have work experience in graphic design or photography studios. These can provide a rich resource of first-hand contact that may be relevant to your own work.

Your contextual material might also take the form of objects or artefacts from different cultures, times or places. For example, materials such as historical architecture and sculpture have been used to inform the development of ideas in the work of Reinhild Beuther, the subject of the artist's case studies in this chapter. In a similar way, a visit to a museum or a collection might give you an opportunity to investigate cultural objects that could provide possible starting points, but might also inform the development of your ideas. In Reinhild's work it is the atmosphere of the ancient cathedral, as well as the visual language of the building and its sculptures, that inform the development of her work.

> ### ■ Remember
>
> ■ You can use contextual material from different times, periods, traditions and cultures.
>
> ■ Do not unnecessarily restrict your contextual material to art of the past.
>
> ■ What about investigating contemporary artists and designers as well?

💡 Case study 10

Using contextual material in Fine Art

Stuart's work, based on different approaches to the representation of the human head, demonstrates how the ideas and techniques of different artists can be used to inform your own practice. Initially, an intriguing image of 'lovers' by René Magritte generated a series of studies related to the theme of concealment. The student also looked at different forms of 'wrapping' used by Christo and the ways that masks were used in different cultures to conceal identity.

In other aspects of his work Stuart made studies of the paintings and drawings of Auerbach and Giacometti. These focused more directly on technique and the handling of materials. In a series of expressive studies the student is able to link the work of the two artists and demonstrate a growing awareness of the different ways in which they have engaged with the figure in space.

A diverse range of contextual materials were used as starting points for developments in the student's own work. They generated a number of possible ideas and a better understanding of the importance of technique.

Fig. 1.45 *René Magritte, The Lovers, 1928*

Fig. 1.46 *Study from Magritte*

Fig. 1.47 *Influence of Auerbach*

Fig. 1.48 *Drawing process*

Fig. 1.49 *Informed by Giacometti*

Fig. 1.50 *The figure and space, a study after Giacometti*

Locating contextual material

For books, magazines, periodicals and exhibition catalogues use the following resources:

- ■ the art department library
- ■ the school library
- ■ local libraries.

On the internet use:

- ■ search engines
- ■ gallery and museum websites
- ■ artists' and designers' own websites.

Most towns have a municipal art gallery and some have private, commercial galleries showing work by contemporary artists. Your local authority website and regional arts organisation should have details of libraries and galleries and lists of practising artists and craftspeople in your area. A Level students frequently show evidence of enthusiasm and motivation stimulated by seeing art first hand, and where this is reflected in their work it can have great value.

■ Link

For more information on art galleries in the U.K. and around the World see www.artinfo.com

Using contextual material to inform the development of your work

There are many ways in which you can respond to contextual material so that it can inform the development of your ideas, depending on the type of material you have collected and your reasons for selecting it.

- ■ Visual analysis, making drawings and colour studies from the work of other artists, could give you an insight into their work because it should make you look closely at aspects of composition and design, colour combinations, a range of different responses to the same kind of subject or source material, techniques and handling of media and processes.
- ■ Looking at works that are appropriate to your own ideas and intentions, bringing images together in a purposeful, deliberate way so that you can make connections between them.
- ■ Responding to contextual material by applying aspects of a work's colour and tone using a different medium and process, for example by reinterpreting an abstract painting of a landscape into fabric, using dyeing or fabric painting techniques and stitch.

Case study 11

Using contextual material to inform different elements of your work in Fine Art

Dasal researched and made reference to a number of artists whose work informed his investigation and the development of his ideas. The contextual material he selected shows some diversity as different artists informed various aspects of his work. He explored Constable's studies of clouds and his paintings from Hampstead Heath (see Figures 1.51 and 1.52) in which atmospheric and highly charged skies and cloud formations are painted expressively. In these works Dasal looked at colour and tone, but particularly at the ways in which the paint and brush strokes are handled. He looked at ways in which Turner expressed light, especially the difficult range of colour in sunsets in works such as *The Fighting Temeraire*.

Fig. 1.51 *Constable*, Hampstead, looking towards Harrow, *date unknown*

Dasal found the series of soft, blurred cloud paintings by Gerhard Richter (see Figure 1.53) interesting, but it was perhaps the works of Anselm Kiefer (see Figure 1.55) and Peter Lanyon (see Figure 1.57) that informed his work to the greatest extent.

Fig. 1.52 *Contextual material*

Fig. 1.53 *Gerhard Richter,* Wolken (Clouds), *1978*

Fig. 1.54 *Acrylic studies*

Fig. 1.55 *Anselm Kiefer,* Nigredo, *1984*

Fig. 1.56 *Watercolour study*

Dasal was drawn to the expressive, abstract qualities in Kiefer's handling of paint in response to the landscape, especially in the grooves and channels of a ploughed field. Both of these elements of Kiefer's work had a profound effect on the ways in which Dasal explored and manipulated his work in response to his source material, prompting him to think in depth and reflect on the direction of his ideas. Kiefer's work informed the ways in which Dasal developed his response to the sky and cloud formations and experimented with the expressive possibilities of paint handling.

Peter Lanyon's work also had a substantial effect in informing Dasal's ideas and it was Lanyon that he chose to study in the written element of Unit 3. Dasal was enthusiastic about the ways in which Lanyon constructed the paint surface in layers and with broad, gestural marks that reveal the journey of the work and the process of his decision making. Lanyon's decision to explore the possibilities of an extended rectangle of double square proportions and his intention to try to re-enact the act of looking, were significant elements in the development of Dasal's own work. He explored various proportions and decided to extend the rectangle of his canvas to intensify the sensation of looking down, across and upwards. Lanyon's painting, *Lost Mine*, and the series of landscapes developed from his gliding experiences, such as *Silent Coast*, were especially significant.

Dasal also made reference to Peter Lanyon's drawing in which lines have an active role in connecting elements of the composition, taking the viewer's eye on a journey. This informed aspects of Dasal's drawing and also elements of his painting.

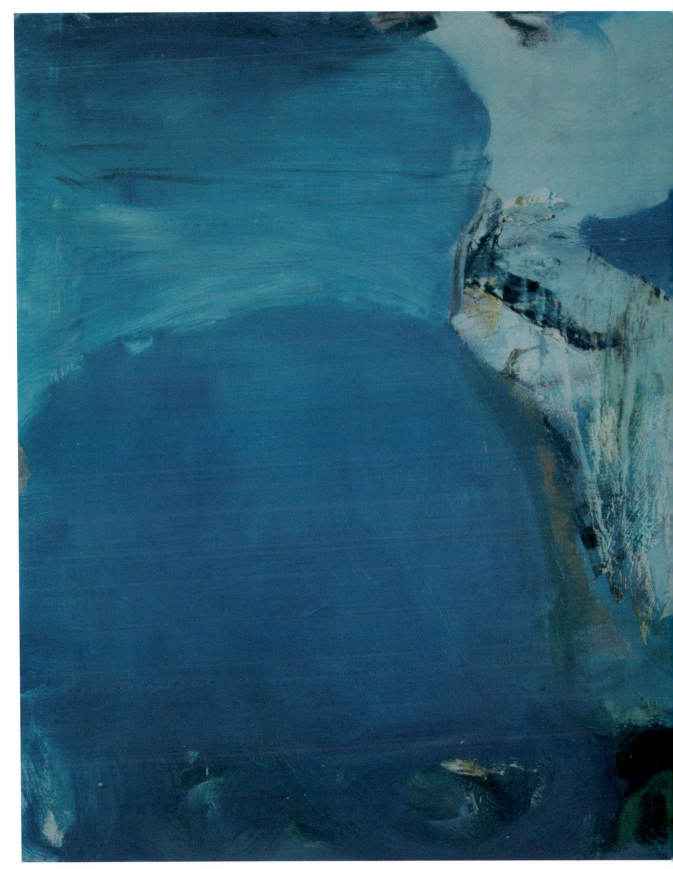

Fig. 1.57 *Peter Lanyon,* Silent Coast, *1957*

Link

For more ideas about media, materials and processes see Chapter 2.

AQA Examiner's tip

Select a range of appropriate contextual materials and decide which will best inform the development of your own work.

Case study 12

Using contextual material in Three-Dimensional Design

The development of ideas in Michael's AS Unit 2 is informed by various forms of contextual material. He has researched examples of sculpture located in existing town sites and has made reference to the work of Santiago Calatrava and Gehry Partners. In addition, Michael has collected and responded to images of bridge structures and tensioned cables.

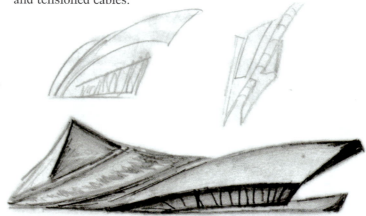

Fig. 1.59 *Sketchbook page*

Selecting contextual material

When investigating contextual sources you might select materials only from within your specialist area of study. Alternatively, you might make reference to work from other areas of art, craft or design. For example, a project in textiles might link to aspects of the coast and the seashore and you could choose to explore a series of marine paintings or marine photography to investigate colour and texture, perhaps making colour studies in coloured pencil and watercolour or gouache, or enhancing and manipulating them using computer software. The results of these studies could inform the process of developing your ideas by informing your exploration of colour and texture.

Case study 13

An artist using contextual material in Photography

Reinhild Beuther studied the History of Art and she has always had a keen interest in the early Middle Ages, especially Romanesque architecture and sculpture. Her ideas are informed by the work of other artists, including Rembrandt, and her knowledge of the History of Art. In *Uta van Naumburg*, Reinhild's knowledge of the Middle Ages informed the development of her ideas. Contextual material included the visual language, characteristics and atmosphere of Naumburg Cathedral's architecture and a group of sculptures that she found there.

Fig. 1.60 *Gerburg*

Fig. 1.61 *Naumburg Cathedral: Northside*

Fig. 1.62 *Hermann and Regelindis*

Using contextual material to inform ideas

In case study 9, Nick's response to water, ripples and movement was informed by his investigation of paintings by Monet and Seurat, in which water is a prominent element. He recorded his observations in annotations. He also investigated contextual material in the form of logo designs and van livery design. These informed the way in which he approached the development of his ideas, by helping him to develop his design concept, as well as directing his attention to the problems of handling space and layout for the van livery design.

In case study 10, Stuart investigated Magritte and Christo and Jeanne-Claude whose work stimulated his thinking around his chosen idea. He also investigated the work of Auerbach and Giacometti in which he had identified ways of responding to the figure and ways of handling media that were appropriate to the development of his own work. Stuart made some studies from these in which he analysed technique and drawing process. He then applied these directly to studies from his own source material.

In case study 11, Dasal investigated the work of a number of artists. He studied ways in which Constable's oil sketches explored broody, powerful, atmospheric skies and cloud formations, with the expressive, painterly handling of oil paint, and the way that Turner expressed light and atmosphere. He also looked at Gerhard Richter's soft, blurred images of clouds, the painterly qualities of Anselm Kiefer's ploughed fields and the aerial paintings of Peter Lanyon. He made a series of small painted studies from several of these in which he looked at colour, tone and paint

Fig. 1.63 *Christo and Jeanne-Claude Wrapped Monument to Vittorio Emanuele, Piazza Duomo, Milano, Italy, 1970 © Christo and Jeanne-Claude*

handling. Each of these was appropriate to the development of Dasal's idea, the problem he gave himself and the way that he chose to approach it in paint and through drawing.

In case study 12, Michael investigated contextual material in several forms, finding different types of images in books and on the internet. These included examples of sculpture and 3D constructions in public spaces as well as architecture by Santiago Calatrava and examples of bridges.

Analysing contextual material

In analysing and exploring contextual material visually, you might, for example, make drawings or colour studies that might inform your understanding of technique or colour and tone, the artist's handling of composition, space and scale. A tracing of the main lines in an image, on tracing paper or on an acetate overlay, might increase your understanding of the artist's handling of composition, space and scale. A study in coloured pencil or paint could give insights into paint handling and technique, the intricacies of colour and tonal values. A charcoal study from a piece of sculpture could increase your understanding and awareness of form, mass and volume, which could influence the way you see and manipulate these elements in your own work.

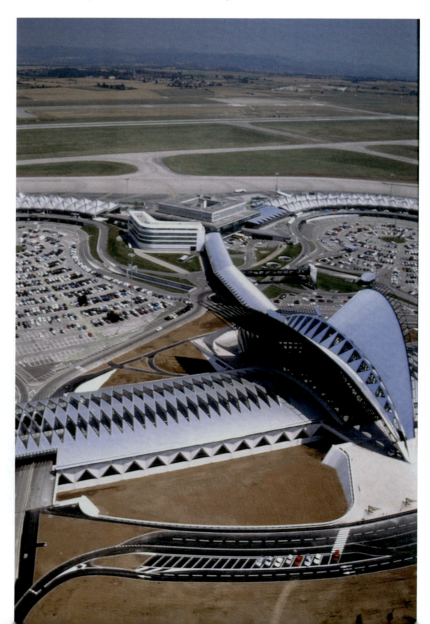

Fig. 1.64 *Lyon-Satolas, France. Santiago Calatrava 1989–94*

The development of analytical and critical thinking

Demonstrating analytical and critical understanding

Analytical and **critical understanding** can be demonstrated in both visual and written work:

- in the way that one image leads to developments in others
- in annotations and in writing
- in sustained in-depth analysis and comparison in the written element of the personal investigation.

Fig. 1.65 *Cape Wrath: © Iain Stewart*

Practical work

Analytical drawings and colour studies need sustained observation that will enable you to explore and discover the characteristics of your source material. Analysis suggests detailed examination and working in depth, demonstrating more than just surface qualities.

In your practical work you can demonstrate critical understanding in various ways:

- in how you use a **visual vocabulary** with understanding and appropriateness
- in the way that one image leads to developments in others
- in the way that one image can be clearly linked to another
- a series of closely related images can demonstrate the development of an idea

■ positioning an image made by yourself alongside that of an appropriate artist, designer or craftsperson might reveal the influence they have had on your work.

■ **Link**

See Chapter 2 for ideas on evaluation and experimenting with media.

■ **Did you know?**

■ Analytical skill and understanding can be demonstrated in both practical and written work.

■ Analytical studies can focus on particular aspects of your source material, line or tone, for example.

Analytical skill can also be shown in analysing your ideas as well as compositional and design problems. It is closely connected to reflection and evaluation.

You will analyse issues such as content, angle and viewpoint, composition, design or layout and the results of media experimentation, in order to evaluate and make decisions about the direction that you can take the work and the changes or refinements you will make. This analytical process might be purely visual or it could be supported with annotations.

Analytical studies can be made in a wide range of media and with a range of intentions and applications. Each study that you make from your source material may aim to explore and obtain a range of visual information, or you may choose to focus on particular aspects.

For example, in making a series of analytical studies, a painter, a printmaker and a sculptor might each demonstrate their analytical and critical understanding in different ways and with different intentions.

■ The painter might look at portraiture and characterisation or the figure in space.

■ The printmaker might look at line, shape, surface and colour.

■ The sculptor might look at form, mass, volume and space.

■ The textile designer might look for line, shape, texture, pattern and decoration.

■ The 3D designer might look at aspects of form, function and materials.

■ The graphic designer might look at images, typography, surface, layout, colour and tone.

■ The photographer might look at composition, depth and space, light and tonal contrasts.

Analytical and critical understanding can be demonstrated in different media, not necessarily through drawing. For example, the sculptor, ceramicist and 3D designer might demonstrate analytical and critical understanding in three-dimensional work, maquettes and models. The photographer might demonstrate it in lens-based activity, by analysing through the lens, in making and analysing contact prints, in analysing ideas and planning a sequence of images or by designing a storyboard. The graphic designer might use digital media and software to analyse images, typography and layout.

Annotations

In case study 9, Nick, the graphic communication student, analysed paintings by Monet and Seurat by simple line drawings because he was primarily interested in the single aspect of the shapes in moving water. In other forms of contextual material that included logo designs and van livery designs, this graphics example demonstrates that it is not always possible to make visual analytical studies from sources.

This is most obviously true in the case of Photography where there might be little to be gained from making a drawn or painted study from a photo image unless you were using drawing to reflect on a compositional problem or to plan a sequence of images. Although the specification in Art and Design requires a written response only in Unit 3, sometimes it may be helpful to record observations in written form in order to make your intentions clear. In case study 9, Nick has supported his photos and line drawings with brief annotations that explain his intentions.

If you choose to use annotations to make your intentions clear, in written work or on audio tapes, you should demonstrate analytical and critical understanding by making a **critical response** rather than being just descriptive. Critical response itself is a difficult term. It does not mean that you are expected to criticise or necessarily find fault with your own work or that of others.

Written material has little purpose if it simply becomes a laborious labelling exercise that adds little to the understanding of the work. Unnecessary or poorly presented written material can ruin preparatory sheets.

If you choose to include annotations they should:

- be meaningful
- explain decisions that you have made
- add to the understanding of aspects of your work or the work of others
- explain processes you have used that would not otherwise be obvious.

Link

See Chapter 3 for ideas about recording your observations and ideas.

Key terms

Critical response: responding in a structured, well-focused way that shows depth of understanding, informed opinions and ideas, rather than just describing surface appearance.

Remember

Unnecessary and badly presented annotations can ruin preparatory sheets.

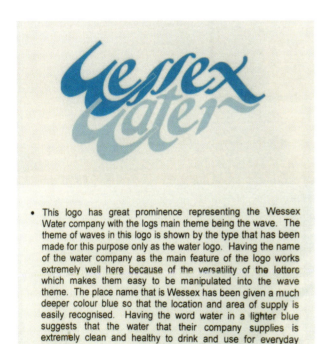

- This logo has great prominence representing the Wessex Water company with the logs main theme being the wave. The theme of waves in this logo is shown by the type that has been made for this purpose only as the water logo. Having the name of the water company as the main feature of the logo works extremely well here because of the versatility of the letters which makes them easy to be manipulated into the wave theme. The place name that is Wessex has been given a much deeper colour blue so that the location and area of supply is easily recognised. Having the word water in a lighter blue suggests that the water that their company supplies is extremely clean and healthy to drink and use for everyday purposes.

Fig. 1.66 *Annotation in Graphic Communication*

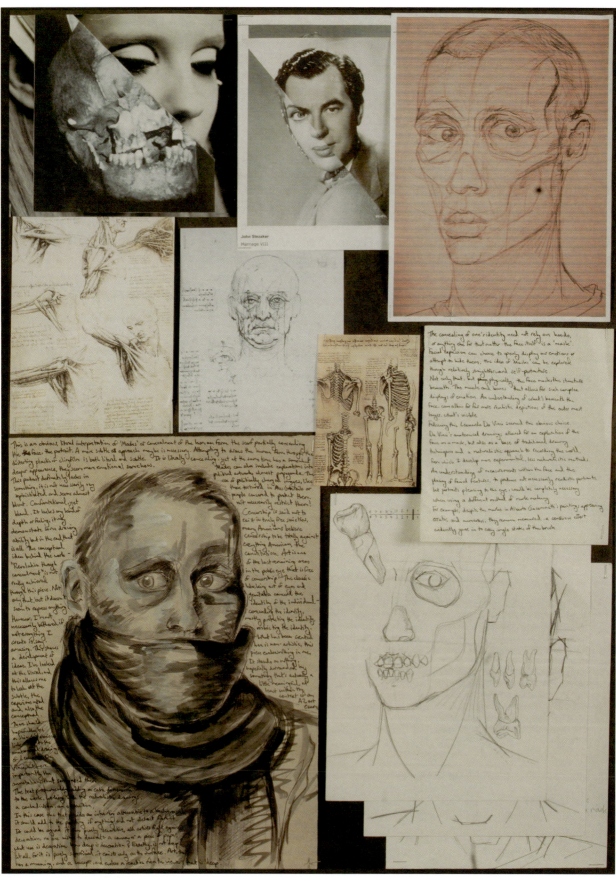

Fig. 1.67 *Fine Art study sheet*

Demonstrating analytical and critical understanding in written work

In Unit 3, the personal investigation, you are required to link visual and written elements of the work. Whatever form your response takes, the writing should show evidence of analytical and critical understanding. Whether analysing or reflecting on practical elements of the unit or on contextual material it should be clear, coherent and accurate, and should demonstrate your understanding of specialist terms. It should also demonstrate your ability to develop ideas rather than being purely descriptive.

The written element of the personal investigation can take different forms, such as:

- written material of a critical, analytical nature in which you will provide insights into and reflect upon aspects of your practical work
- a personal study based on an aspect of art, craft or design practice.

Fig. 1.68 *Preparatory study*

Written reflection of 1,000–3,000 words

Your writing should provide insights into:

■ your intentions

■ influences on the development of your work

■ your reasons for making decisions.

Reports on visits to galleries or studios and workshops might form part of this work and you must include an analytical and critical evaluation of your practical work. The written work should be carefully constructed and thoughtfully presented. It must show evidence of your ability to use analytical and critical skills which could be demonstrated in the way that you:

■ analyse your own work and the work of others

■ make comparisons and connections

■ analyse techniques and processes

■ develop ideas

■ use **specialist terms** and **critical vocabulary** appropriately and accurately.

Fig. 1.69 *Preparatory studies*

Personal study of 1,000–3,000 words

The more formal personal study is an alternative approach in which the writing is carried out alongside your practical work and is linked to it so that the personal study informs and supports the practical project. It should provide evidence of your ability to analyse and evaluate works by relevant artists, designers, craftspeople and photographers using specialist terms and critical vocabulary with appropriateness and accuracy.

Whether you are analysing painting or sculpture, examples of Graphic Communication, textiles, Three-Dimensional Design or Photography, your analyses of contextual material, in written form, need to be well organised and thoughtfully put together. In the course of the project you might analyse complete works but you might also choose some examples, to focus on a particular aspect or feature. Demonstrate critical understanding in the way that you use a critical vocabulary to analyse and compare works.

Analysis of an image or object could include your observations on all or some of the following visual elements:

- line
- shape
- tone
- colour
- form, mass, volume
- size and scale
- space
- texture and surface
- media and techniques
- composition and design.

The terms given to these visual elements form the basis of a critical vocabulary that you will use to express your observations in words and demonstrate your critical understanding.

■ Remember

Demonstrate your ability to develop ideas through a sustained and focused investigation.

AQA Examiner's tip

Demonstrate your ability to analyse and compare.

💡 Case study 14

Analytical and critical understanding in written work for Fine Art

In his practical work for Unit 3, Dasal developed his ideas informed by the work of a number of artists that included Constable, Turner, Anselm Kiefer, Gerhard Richter and Peter Lanyon. The written work focuses on aspects of Lanyon's paintings that are especially relevant to Dasal's own work.

Lanyon's painting informed the development of Dasal's ideas in his practical work. He gained insight into process, paint layers, the notion of time and the possibilities of exploring image-making by stretching the proportions of the canvas to an elongated rectangle. This makes the spectator look down, across towards the horizon and up to the sky, eventually suggesting looking overhead. He also developed an element of ambiguity in his work where, as a spectator, we are uncertain whether we are looking at an image of a dramatic sky or at a landscape and the layers of ground beneath its surface.

In his personal study, Dasal wrote: 'In this final version of *St Just*, there are visible signs of the thick, heavy layering of impasto paint that Lanyon built up during his reworking, and his development of a more painterly handling is demonstrated. Instead of the more usual white surface of the primed canvas, Lanyon probably painted this work on a black 'ground', an underlayer of black paint, and this affects both colour and tonal values, which adds a sense of drama to the painting. He uses the extended rectangle of the canvas to intensify the feeling of the dark labyrinth of underground mine tunnels beneath the landscape, which takes our eyes on a journey from the surface, the Cornish landscape, to the darkness and depths of the subterranean mines'.

Fig. 1.70 *Study in chalk and watercolour*

Fig. 1.71 *Study in acrylic paint*

Having read this chapter you should now be able to:

- select an idea, issue or theme for which you can gather appropriate resources
- explore and sustain an in-depth investigation
- consider alternative ideas and approaches in developing your ideas
- use contextual and other sources to inform the development of your own work
- demonstrate analytical and critical understanding in both practical and written elements of your work.

Fig. 2.1 *A textiles project*

The selection of resources, media and materials appropriate to your intentions will enable you to develop your ideas. To do this, you will need to know *what* media are available to you, their characteristics, and *how* to use them.

Experimentation and experience should help to develop your understanding of the characteristics of media. The success of a project depends upon your developing a working familiarity with media and materials and developing skills in their use. Experimenting with media and techniques that are appropriate to your work will enable you to explore lines of enquiry in your investigations of source material and in developing your ideas. Your use of media will also enable you to review and refine your ideas as your work develops.

■ Selecting appropriate resources to develop ideas and intentions

How do you start to select what to use to develop your work? Reference to contextual materials, examples by other artists and designers, can help to set a course and direction for a project, and you should also experiment with media and images by, for example, exploring and responding to your source material using a range of different media and techniques. For example, one of your photographs could be interpreted in water-colour to see the possibilities of softer more fluid tones or colours, or into **collage** to explore textures and broader sweeps of colour areas.

Source material

Your source material can be explored using a range of media, methods and techniques appropriate to your area of study, to express its visual and tactile qualities or other characteristics that you have seen.

Your studies could include a range of different approaches and intentions. The visual elements of shape, form, scale and proportion, colour, texture, pattern and decoration, harmony and contrast pervade all art and design disciplines and you should demonstrate an appropriate understanding and application of the principles of organisation and composition of these elements in your work.

Case study 15, for example, shows how observations made from structures in modern architecture can be developed into a dress through different media experiments using photography, collage, drawing, printing and mock-ups.

💡 Case study 15

Selecting resources to develop ideas in Textile Design

The Textile Design Unit 4, externally set assignment, comprises eight A2 size mounts of studies, an A4 sketchbook and a fabric and mixed media dress that was produced in the 15 hour period of supervised time. The starting point is 'Structures' and the media used range from photography and drawing as recording methods, to prints (digital, mono and screen), collage, and a range of textiles construction and embellishment methods through which ideas are developed.

In response to the theme, Alex has taken photographs of the London Eye which she has responded to, using a range of materials

---

In this chapter you will learn how to:

- ■ develop your knowledge and understanding of media, materials, processes and techniques

- ■ develop skills to select and experiment with resources, media and materials

- ■ develop skills in handling media and techniques

- ■ develop skills and understanding in making images and artefacts

- ■ use media and techniques to review and refine ideas as your work develops.

■ Key terms

Collage: an image made by pasting together assembled fragments of paper or other materials, 'discovered' by Picasso and Braque in the early 20th century.

■ Links

See Chapter 1 for more ideas about using contextual materials.

See Chapter 3 for more ideas about recording your observations and insights.

AQA Examiner's tip

In making reference to contextual material, demonstrate your understanding.

■ Remember

Textile Design candidates should produce practical and critical/contextual work in one or more areas including fashion, printed and/or dyed fabrics and materials, domestic textiles, wallpaper, interior design, constructed textiles and installed textiles.

This Alexander McQueen dress is another of his structural triumphs. It is strikingly feminine with a hooped skirt and power shoulders, however with the garment being left to the bare skin and bones it has an unfinished quality that I find disturbing. McQueen's use of prosthetic legs makes the model look like a long discarded manakin for an old fashioned bridal shop!

However, I do think that the hooped skirt is an element for me to consider. If I used doweling in a way similar to this I could create a very structure skirt with far more support than a mere netting tutu would provide.

Fig. 2.2 *Research sheet showing Alex's experiments with printed and pleated fabric*

and techniques, with the aim of 'communicating the intricate structures of The Eye into a wearable piece'. These studies include surface printing, free machining, mixed-media structures, dissolvable fabric, pleating, cutting, tearing and recombining, and **appliqué**. Design layouts and ideas are worked out through Adobe Photoshop, collage, pencil, inks, crayon and fabrics. The decorative surface designs have been reconstructed to create a bodice dress which makes strong links to Miyaki, Chalayan, Wantanabe and McQueen. See Figure 2.2, which is a research sheet showing McQueen's dress and Alex's experiments with printed and pleated fabric, and Figure 2.3, which shows photo-printed images on paper and fabric with accompanying drawings in pen and paint exploring design motifs.

Did you know?

■ Photo screen printing is a 20th-century invention.

■ Before Andy Warhol used industrial photo screen printing technology in the 1960s for his artwork, screens were either hand painted or hand-cut stencils were used. One of his printed portraits of Elizabeth Taylor was sold in 2007 for over £20 million.

Key terms

Appliqué: literally work laid or applied onto another surface – usually fabrics, lace, etc.

Fig. 2.3 *Study sheet of motifs in print and drawing*

Finding appropriate media

Case study 15 shows how you should be selective in your use of media and processes. Alex shows how she has incorporated both contextual and secondary sources into her work. The other case studies in this chapter also provide examples of how students have experimented with a range of media and techniques in developing their ideas. Artists and designers in different disciplines use a wide range of materials and processes, so do not restrict your choice of media without considering how each may be used to develop your own work. Finding the most appropriate medium or media to develop your ideas and intentions, and to respond to your source material, is best achieved by going through a process of experimentation and trying things out.

 ### Case study 16

An artist's selection of appropriate resources and media in Fine Art

Dionne Barber has developed a personal language and approach to painting which is bound up with her choice of media and materials. She records her ideas through sketching in pencil, pen and oil bars as well as using the camera to capture immediate impressions of places and people. The informal, loose character of her drawings and the subsequent reworking and refining of images through a wide range of oil painting techniques are ingredients of her working method.

Fig. 2.4 *Oil bar study by Dionne*

She finds drawing with a pen 'is more immediate' and the oil bars provide a paintlike effect which allows her to start seeing colours, shapes and surfaces in a way that resembles the final qualities of her paintings. When painting, she uses a number of different-sized brushes as well as palette knives, and her oil paint is applied in different consistencies, sometimes thick from the tube or at other times diluted with white spirit. She swaps between application methods, sometimes rubbing colours back with a cloth or manipulating them with her bare hands. She also photographs her work in order to see it on a different scale or 'in a different light'. Her choice of media and techniques makes her work what it is: pictures of architectural forms by day and night become transformed into dynamic images suggesting movement and the passage of time. See Figure 2.5.

Fig. 2.5 *Study by Dionne Barber*

■ Understanding the characteristics and experimenting with media and approaches

It is important to understand that the characteristics of materials can be exploited to express different qualities in your source material. For example, a **line and wash** technique using a fineliner, water and a sable brush will enable you to explore delicate lines and subtleties of tone, whereas charcoal might enable you to express mass, form and volume with strong **tonal contrasts**. The medium can even determine the final form of your work. If you work in clay, your ideas will explore form in real space, but if you use photography your images will be two-dimensional.

Fig. 2.6 *Examples of AS photography*

Before making a final choice of process or medium, you should experiment to discover for yourself what different media and techniques can offer the development of your work. One study in a particular medium could lead to another. For example, an illustration in pencil could be transformed by working in ink and wash on a larger or smaller scale. The linear qualities of the initial study would be extended or enhanced by a study in which tonal values or a sense of form and space are expressed.

In case study 15 the candidate has taken her initial recordings of the London Eye through a detailed development sequence into surface patterns and structural designs for a dress. In case study 17 the student has worked in a broad range of media including watercolour and acrylics, to explore how texture, paint effects and colour may be manipulated and incorporated into layers within the final design. Dionne Barber, our case study artist, is skilled at working with oil-based and acrylic paints of different thicknesses and fluidity, characteristics that significantly affect the final appearance of her work.

Fig. 2.7 *Dionne Barber's use of oil paint*

■ Key terms

Wash: a thin layer of watercolour applied with a broad brush or sponge.

Ground: a first layer of transparent paint applied to watercolour paper or illustration board which establishes a ground colour or shade that will affect the appearance of colours applied later on.

Key colour: a colour that links part of a composition or design, or that creates a link between other colours used in a painting, e.g. red may provide a key between orange tones and blues/purples.

Wet on wet: the method often employed in watercolour painting where colour is flooded into a dampened area of paper or where paint is allowed to bleed into an adjacent area of wet paint, creating a soft area of colour with blurred or bleeding edges.

■ Did you know?

Turner believed in the importance of observing from real life – he travelled extensively throughout Europe in the early 1800s and there is one story that tells of him being roped to the mast of a cross-channel sailing ship during a storm so that he could record the extreme weather! (*Snow Storm – Steam Boat off a Harbour's Mouth*, 1842)

Working with water-based media

In this chapter several of the case studies exemplify ways of working with water-based paint and inks, a readily available and flexible range of media that have been used by some artists and designers to explore, record and develop their ideas. They are useful for quick initial studies to get the feel of source material, to identify and express characteristics of shape, colour and surface, whilst also lending themselves to sustained analytical studies that scrutinise source material in depth.

When used successfully, watercolour can suggest light, volume and space most effectively through transparent or translucent colour. Watercolour painting often needs to be undertaken with confidence and a light touch, and the artist needs to accept and work with the accidental effects that often occur in such a fluid medium.

Some watercolour methods

One way of developing a water-colour study is to draw out the main structure, then experiment with laying in a **wash** by applying a thin layer of a colour to act as a **ground** to work on. Because watercolour is transparent, the wash should be selected carefully as it will influence all of the colours that you apply subsequently. For example, a blue will provide a **key colour** for a landscape that will consist mainly of blues, greens and browns. The same blue for an interior setting in warm colours will make those colours cooler than if a red or terracotta wash is used as a ground. Areas that appear too sharp can be rewashed and 'pulled' (removed or taken back to the base paper colour) with a dry brush or tissue. Care should be taken to avoid making any effect too repetitive or heavy. In Figure 2.8 highlights have been left untouched with colour, allowing the white surface of the paper to show through. This also shows how working **wet on wet** is a technique that can be used to produce a sense of hazy distance and depth.

Fig. 2.8 *J.M.W. Turner,* view over an Alpine Valley, *c. 1841*

Tempera and gouache

Tempera and gouache are heavier, opaque water-based media which can be used to build up an image or design in a similar way to watercolour but which have the advantage of providing stronger colours and tones if desired. Designers often use gouache because of the refined quality of its pigment and for the way in which it can be used to produce flat, uniform layers of colour. Images may be drawn out in detail in pencil, then washes are applied, allowed to dry and then additional colours are built up. Alternatively opaque colour may be applied directly to provide richer, saturated colour effects or dense tonal values.

A range of these painting techniques and methods can be seen in case study 17.

 ## Case study 17

Experimenting with media and approaches in Graphic Communication

In response to an externally set assignment starting point that required designs for playing cards based on nursery rhymes, Esperant worked through an extremely thorough series of more than 30 A2 size design sheets. These explore different types of images which are drawn or painted then scanned, layered and manipulated using ICT and software programs including Adobe Photoshop and Cinema 4D. Images are juxtaposed in a variety of combinations and media including pencil, ink, crayon, watercolour, tempera and acrylic paint, collage and printmaking methods.

Fig. 2.9 *Research sheet: references to Elliot Thoburn*

Fig. 2.10 *Study sheet on the theme of 'Three blind mice'*

Esperant found a range of examples of graphic designers' work which he felt could inform the development of his ideas. These include contemporary paintings by Malone, graphic illustrations by Thoburn, White and Navascues (see Figure 2.9). He has shown his understanding of their various styles and techniques through his sketches and studies. Responding in a different medium on a new scale provides Esperant's work with a sense of development. Even in the early stages of work it should be possible to start developing your own ideas and experimenting with media, as can be seen in the drawings in Figures 2.10 and 2.11.

Remember

Acknowledge your contextual sources.

Fig. 2.11 *… and 'Row your boat'*

Fig. 2.12 *Studies from contextual material, Edwina White*

Fig. 2.13 *Study sheet: Combined images created in Photoshop*

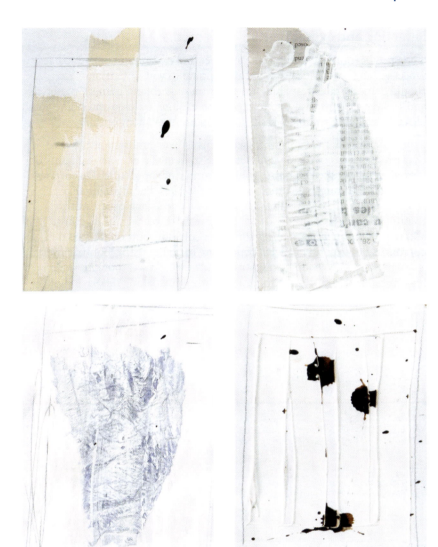

Fig. 2.14 *Study sheet: experimenting with media and techniques*

After researching playing-card designs, he experimented with backgrounds in a range of media using paint, collage, line and wash. Esperant shows that he understands the potential and characteristics of the media he uses. Each study is worked in a different colour combination in order to develop the images further. See Figure 2.14 where paint textures and splashed inks create an informal and visually interesting background for further design ideas, and Figure 2.15 where washed and dragged paint areas are combined with collage to create interesting surface textures.

Techniques used include:

■ watercolour which is applied wet on wet, wet on dry and then washed from one edge

■ collaged newspaper and acrylic paint in layers

■ ink drawing is washed and spattered.

Some of Esperant's studies were scanned into the computer. Using Adobe Photoshop, he overlaid images from different sources to visualise how colour and texture could be combined in both front and back designs for the cards.

Key terms

Monotype: also known as monoprint, a simple method of making direct or indirect prints by drawing directly onto an inked-up plate or drawing on the back of a sheet of paper placed on an inked plate.

Collatype: a method of making direct prints by inking up an image made from surface textures or cut or torn cardboard or paper.

AQA Examiner's tip

Refine your control and selection of different media and techniques as your ideas develop.

Selecting and experimenting with media

The Specification encourages you to select and experiment with media, processes and techniques that are appropriate to your intentions. You should demonstrate your ability to experiment with and manage materials and techniques effectively, so that you can explore, develop and refine your ideas. Developing technical skill is an important element of this.

Think about how media can be used to investigate and respond to the characteristics of your source material, or to help you explore and focus on formal elements such as mass, volume, form, line or texture. Discoveries can be made through sustained, analytical studies, but it might also be appropriate to experiment with accidental effects achieved through techniques such as staining, dripping, scratching, tearing, or layering and manipulating images using computer software. You might find it appropriate to experiment with combining media or using 'non-traditional' art materials such as food dyes, string, pulverised brick, soil and sand, broken slate, or you might experiment with printmaking media and techniques such as **monotype** or **collatype** to help develop your ideas.

Fig. 2.15 *Study sheet: surface textures*

Experimenting with techniques and processes

Experimenting not just with materials but also with techniques may help you to explore and develop your ideas and your response to your source material. It may also provide some dramatic images for further exploration and development.

For example, you might experiment with and explore **negative space** by drawing the shapes and spaces 'in between' solid forms, such as the negative spaces between railings, tree branches or between a figure and the surrounding space. Negative space is an important concept not only in painting and sculpture but also in areas of study such as Graphic Communication, especially in developing ideas for page layout and when combining images with type.

AQA **Examiner's tip**

Explore how ideas, feelings and meanings can be conveyed through different working methods.

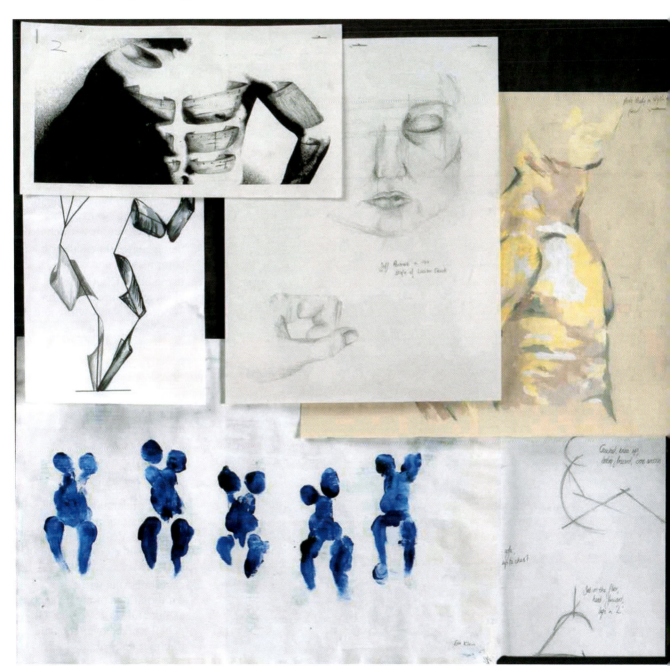

Fig. 2.16 *A range of studies in different media*

Fig. 2.17 *Drawing using mixed media*

Methods and techniques for developing ideas and images

Other ways in which the selection of methods and techniques can contribute to the 'journey' of development might include:

■ drawing in white ink on a dark ground so that your attention is on observing highlights rather than shadows

■ line and wash

■ placing the emphasis on tonal values

■ expressing extreme contrasts in a limited range of black, grey and white tones

■ using biro, fineliner or pen

■ using Indian ink, drawing with an ink dropper, eye dropper, sticks of various thicknesses, feathers, a rolled up leaf, etc.

■ using charcoal, lay down an even charcoal ground using the edge of a charcoal stick and cotton wool. Wipe highlights into it using a putty rubber and work back into it with charcoal

■ using charcoal pencils and compressed charcoal

■ using black Conté crayon: black and white; black, brown and white; black, white and greys

■ using chalk pastel or pastel pencils

■ using oil pastel

■ using coloured pencils

■ experimenting with ink drawing and wax resist over a layered colour base. See Figure 2.19 where a Henry Moore sketchbook page from 1950 shows how the artist's understanding and experimentation with the characteristics of a medium enhances the development of ideas

■ experimenting with combinations of media such as ink and white acrylic, HB pencil worked over gouache, fineliner and watercolour

- experimenting with different types of paper to work on such as newsprint, brown wrapping paper, etc.
- distressing the paper surface with correction fluid, white emulsion, diluted PVA, torn and creased paper, and working over it
- scanning your images or artwork and using software to manipulate them. Experiment with cropping, filters, layers, colour, tonal values, etc.
- experimenting with shutter speeds, aperture settings, and darkroom techniques
- working with clay to devise pot forms by stretching or distorting slabs, coils and bars and then drawing from these forms to investigate their potential for both two- and three-dimensional designs.

Case study 18 is a good example of a student understanding how to experiment with her chosen media. She has combined techniques and processes to develop her line of thinking, creating an original and dramatic sequence of studies leading to her final outcome.

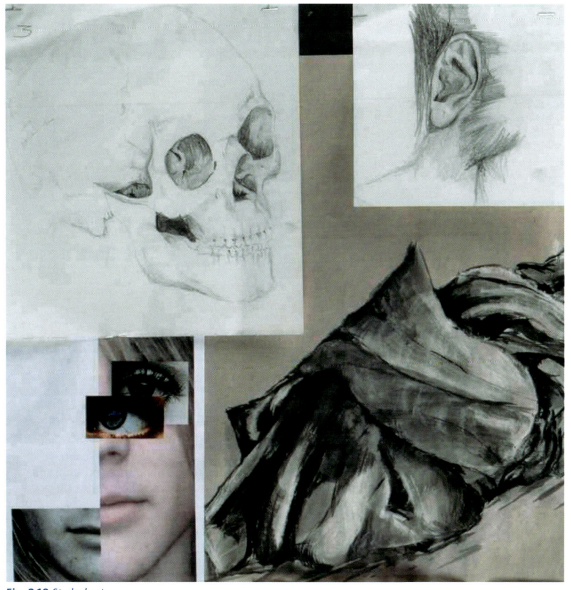

Fig. 2.18 *Study sheet*

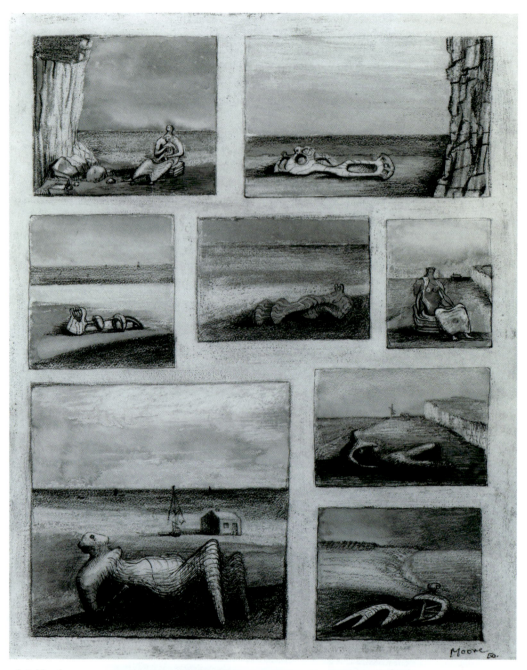

Fig. 2.19 *Henry Moore sketchbook page from 1950*

Experimenting with media and approaches in Textile Design

Early sketchbook studies from Alex's photos of The Eye explore changes of photographic imagery and design through contrast and colour enhancements using Adobe Photoshop, printing onto tracing paper, building textured surfaces and layers with threads, watercolour and line drawings. Close analysis of chosen contextual sources through fabric samples worked to create similar effects to McQueen and Comme des Garçons collections is supported by annotations that are helpful, informative and understanding: 'patches of ruffles appear throughout patterned fabrics' and 'I could … combine ruffles with a structured screen print … and pleats'.

Throughout this project Alex has experimented with printmaking methods, drawing, collage, textiles techniques and construction methods, and her work is focussed and sustained. Figure 2.20 shows source photos, fabric samples, prints and annotations which are presented as a densely worked collection of ideas in a range of media. Case study 23 describes and illustrates in detail her working methods.

Fig. 2.20 *Study sheet: experiments in a range of media*

Experimenting with photography

For many artists, photography is becoming an increasingly common and popular way of recording initial observations, and this can be seen in Dionne Barber's working process. Figure 2.21 shows her photo of a city street and the accompanying compositional study for a painting.

AQA **Examiner's tip**

Any photos that you present in your development work should demonstrate selection and control.

Fig. 2.21 *Dionne Barber sketchbook page*

If you decide to use photography as a means of recording and then experimenting with images, you need to remember that it is a potentially powerful and complex medium with many subtleties and opportunities for selection and control. It is relatively easy to point a digital camera at a subject and simply print off the resulting picture. Take the opportunity to demonstrate skills, understanding and the ability to explore the elements of visual language: line, tone, form, colour, pattern and texture.

Principles of successful photography

Photography is about looking and seeing, and good photography is characterised by controlled composition, colour and lighting – with the most important element initially being framing. A great subject can be weakened or lost completely if the image is poorly framed or structured. Many artists and photographers employ the rule of thirds which is a geometric means of balancing a composition by placing subjects or focal points in a scene either one-third or two-thirds across the **picture plane**.

Composition

A well-composed photograph often contains a level horizon with vertical and horizontal structures included within the frame to create a sense of balance. Figure 2.22 shows a carefully composed image which has the strong vertical elements of the tower set against softer horizontal features such as silhouetted trees and buildings. The clouds and distant horizon add a dramatic sense of depth.

Photographers sometimes choose to ignore or contradict principles of composition to create a more stylised, expressive or dramatic image.

Viewpoints

Carefully selected viewpoints, interesting vantage points, low angles, close-ups, are all important parts of the language of image making, and you should experiment with these at every opportunity. Some of Dionne Barber's photographs are blurred or tilted to convey a sense of moving through a cityscape. The immediacy and spontaneity of such informal compositions can be a rich source of ideas, for example in Figure 2.23 where a long exposure at night creates light trails and Figure 2.24 where a painting in its early stages demonstrates similar visual qualities.

Fig. 2.22 *Photograph from case study 4 AS portfolio*

Fig. 2.23 *Examples of creating light trails in a photo*

Fig. 2.24 *Early stages of a painting by Dionne*

Lighting

Lighting is an important element in photography. The time of day, seasons and weather all influence how a scene or object appears to us. Control of the patterns or play of light and tonal range in a photo requires a strong understanding of camera controls. **Shutter speed**, **aperture** and the use of flash as infill are dealt with at length in a wide range of technical manuals on both film and **digital photography**. Figure 2.25 shows a workbook page where three images demonstrate careful selection of subject which, when combined with good natural lighting conditions and controlled exposure, creates a strong photograph.

Fig. 2.25 *Workbook page from case study 19*

Fig. 2.26 *Workbook page from case study 19*

Recording movement

A sense of motion through blurring in parts of your image can be achieved either by following a fast-moving subject with your camera or by setting a slow shutter speed and keeping the camera still as the subject moves past you. Figure 2.27 illustrates different ways of creating a sense of movement in a photograph, using a slow shutter speed or jogging the camera to produce blurs.

Further characteristics

It is also important to remember that:

- Zoomed pictures may appear flattened, whilst wide-angle shots can exaggerate a sense of depth, perspective and angles. Careful selection of lens as well as camera settings is important.
- Photographers have often used black and white rather than colour as a means of creating a particular mood in their images, or to provide a sense of **documentary realism**.

You could also consider the opportunities offered by techniques such as **posterisation** and **solarisation**, in addition to using **test strips**, contact prints and **exposure** to experiment with and advance your ideas.

💡 Case study 19

Understanding the characteristics of Photography

This AS portfolio project is presented in an A3 spiral-bound workbook containing approximately 36 pages of digital and **wet process photographs** documenting Manchester. Photographs range in size from approximately A6 to A4 and use both colour and black and white. Contextual links are made to Friedlander and Baltz (see Figure 2.28), and to contemporary photographers of Manchester such as Vincent Lowe and Aidan O'Rourke. In his annotations, Yousef has demonstrated an awareness and appreciation of formal elements, composition, viewpoint, lighting and colour, which help him to clarify his intentions. For example: 'I wanted to cram as much urban landscape as I could into a narrow tight space … to represent how crowded cities can get'; 'This photo was cropped to add more focus to the subject … [to] also show the emptiness ... I wanted to show the loneliness that you can … find in busy cities like Manchester'.

Having set out his objectives to 'document the city of Manchester … in abstract … and architectural ways … to present a grim lonely feeling', Yousef has explored a range of different locations and artefacts, aware of camera angles, subject and changes in scale. An understanding of dramatic perspectives, in particular, characterises his work. His annotations also demonstrate a clear understanding of the characteristics of the medium: 'the worm's eye view gives the building a powerful quality … like a hero almost'. And in Figure 2.29 it can be seen how 'the larger aperture helped create a shallower depth of field and draw the eye' to particular areas of the images: on the left the lamppost is clear whilst the distant cars appear softer and less important, and on the right the brickwork is blurred in the distance with the focus directed to the graffiti in the foreground.

Fig. 2.27 *Recording movement*

Key terms

Documentary realism: images which document an event, usually with human interest and often focusing on a social issue.

Posterisation: the process of flattening and separating tonal areas of a photograph.

Solarisation: the process of reversing tonal areas so that light tones become dark and dark tones become light.

Test strips: in traditional photography, test strips using full sheets or strips of photographic paper are used to test exposure times, contrast adjustments and processing time.

Exposure: the amount of light allowed onto photographic film, an image sensor or photographic paper.

Wet process photography: a process whereby the camera uses a light-sensitive film which is then chemically treated to produce a negative. The image on this is projected through an enlarger in a darkroom onto light-sensitive paper, which is then processed to make the image appear.

■ Remember

If you choose to make annotations, make certain they are analytical. Do not just describe what you have done.

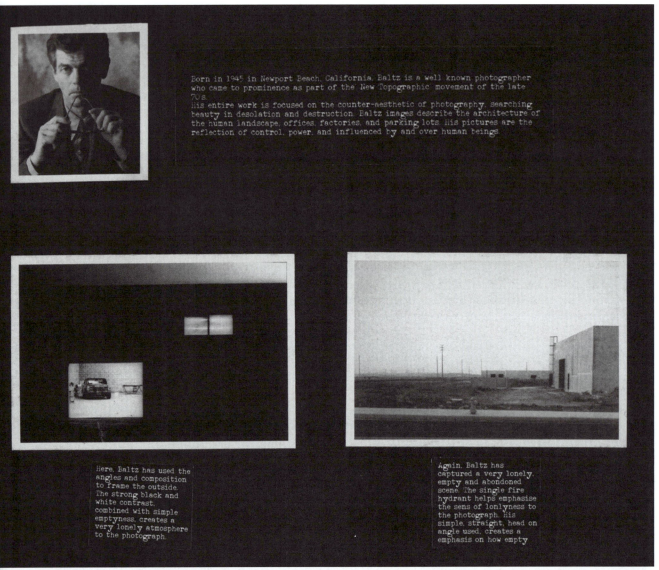

Born in 1945 in Newport Beach, California, Baltz is a well known photographer who came to prominence as part of the New Topographic movement of the late 70's.
His entire work is focused on the counter-aesthetic of photography, searching beauty in desolation and destruction. Baltz images describe the architecture of the human landscape, offices, factories, and parking lots. His pictures are the reflection of control, power, and influenced by and over human beings

Here, Baltz has used the angles and composition to frame the outside. The strong black and white contrast, combined with simple emptyness, creates a very lonely atmosphere to the photograph.

Again, Baltz has captured a very lonely, empty and abondoned scene. The single fire hydrant helps emphasise the sens of lonlyness to the photograph. His simple, straight, head on angle used, creates a emphasis on how empty

Fig. 2.28 *Workbook page: annotations on Baltz*

Fig. 2.29 *Workbook page demonstrating control of focus*

Yousef's images demonstrate his observational skills and clear intentions in developing and resourcing his ideas. His exploration and experimentation with a range of formats and compositions, eye levels and viewpoints, shows evidence of a sustained and focused investigation. It also shows selection and refinement as the work makes progress. Yousef has gone to great lengths to select the best camera angles, as may be seen in Figure 2.30 where an everyday subject is dramatised by the viewpoint. His understanding of the division of space within the picture frame is linked effectively to his contextual sources. In Figure 2.31 the two images make strong connections to Friedlander and Baltz whilst demonstrating his understanding of composition, focus and lighting. Yousef's images are processed using Adobe Photoshop to crop them and to manipulate light and contrast to refine the final outcomes.

Fig. 2.30 *Workbook page showing the importance of viewpoints*

Fig. 2.31 *Photographs connecting to contextual sources*

Key terms

Pushing the medium: an expression that refers to experimenting with a medium or technique, pushing it to its limits, finding out what you can do with it.

AQA Examiner's tip

Your studies should show that you have analysed and evaluated your work as it progresses.

Developing skills in handling media and techniques

Skills in handling media to develop the quality, control and fluency of your work can be developed through practice. By experimenting with media and techniques you will learn how to manage media and discover what they are capable of. Your work should reflect not only the creative journey of investigating and developing ideas but should also demonstrate increasing confidence and competence in the use of your chosen materials.

Experimenting with media, techniques and processes often means **pushing the medium** to see what can be achieved with it, how far you can take it. This could mean working and reworking studies, experimenting, trying different techniques, asking questions of the medium and of yourself. Be prepared to make time to develop your skill and knowledge. Case study 17 demonstrates a strong development of techniques and confidence in using media to explore ideas and designs, whilst case studies 18 and 19 show similarly significant experimentation with all of the visual and tactile elements of their disciplines in order to refine their ideas.

💡 Case study 20

Developing skills in Graphic Communication

In a sequence of study sheets, Esperant has recorded his ideas for illustrating various nursery rhymes. His ideas are explored in pencil and ink drawings that are tinted with watercolour (see Figure 2.31).

Fig. 2.32 *Study sheet*

Fig. 2.33 *Study sheet of layered and combined images formed by contextual material*

Esperant has used Adobe Photoshop to combine images into ideas for three sets of designs that have been informed by contextual material (that includes the work of Edwina White). Sketches and drawings were used to draft ideas and images before developing them using electronic media. Combinations of images in layers can be seen in the process sheets. Cinema 4D has been used to develop depth and form in the images, in contrast with the flatness of earlier ideas (see Figure 2.34). Final designs were produced for both surfaces of a playing card. As the work progressed, Esperant selected a range of appropriate media and techniques that enabled him to develop and refine his ideas.

AQA Examiner's tip

Give thought to how you present your work.

Remember

In this graphics case study, Esperant has used image-enhancing software to refine his images and designs. The tools used are the same as those employed for processing photos in the digital darkroom in case study 22.

Fig. 2.34 *Study sheet showing development of both skills and ideas*

Fig. 2.35 *Cinema4D studies with contextual annotations*

Characteristics of different paints

Acrylic and oil paint present a range of possibilities: oil paint is thick and slow drying, whereas acrylic dries very quickly and tends to lack body. Slow-drying gel can be added to acrylic to allow it to be worked wet into wet, and impasto gel can be added to thicken the paint, giving it more body. Oil paint can be made more fluid by the addition of thinners such as turpentine, and it can be made to dry more quickly with additives. Experimentation with paint consistency and surface effects may be seen in the processes employed by Dionne Barber. In Figure 2.36 she creates a rich surface to the work by building layers into each other.

Painting techniques

If you are using oil paint or acrylic, you might consider the following techniques:

- Body colour is paint which has been given body or opacity by the addition of white. This may be used to provide colour in one layer without depending upon underlying colours for its effect, although skilful combinations of methods can create highly atmospheric and dramatic images. Because body colour is opaque, light reflects from the surface and the colour is perceived as flat without visual depth. If used well some strong images result, but care should be taken that the lack of depth does not deaden the work.

- Scraping back involves laying down an area of colour which is then removed with the edge of a palette knife or brush handle to reveal underlying colours or the texture of the ground.

- Scumbling means to drag paint over the surface of a painting so that it makes irregular or broken traces of colour, which leave the underlying ground or colour surface partly visible.

Did you know?

Acrylic paints became widely available in the 1960s and were created as a substitute for oil-based paints as they were quicker drying and water based, thus making them easier to use.

Fig. 2.36 *Dionne creates a rich surface to her works*

Key terms

Dry brush technique: when a brush loaded with relatively thick paint is gently dragged over the surface of a painting to add a layer of textured colour.

Link

To view more samples of Dionne Barber's work, see www.dionnebarber.com.

Case study 21

An artist's skills in handling media for Fine Art

At university Dionne Barber specialised in painting, gaining a BA(Hons) Fine Art. Currently she works from her studio in Oxfordshire, exhibits widely and has a great deal of experience with residencies and workshops in galleries and schools.

At the start of a painting she energetically covers the canvas with oil paint which is fluid to use and easily manipulated. Dionne always stands when working and has special brushes for different purposes: one for thick oil pigment, another for white spirit and a third for **dry brush technique**. The brushes, always close at hand, are swapped around deftly in order to maintain momentum.

She strives to enhance her skills and to improve communication, and this challenge takes place each time Dionne engages with canvas, paint, brushes and ideas. Experimenting with different ways of applying paint to canvas or board using palette knives, hands, fingers, rags and turpentine has provided her with a variety of mark-making techniques which she employs as required.

Fig. 2.37 *Dionne Barber working on a recent canvas*

Photographic skills – the digital darkroom

If you use photography as a medium to record observations and to resource your work, you can enhance, manipulate and crop images to develop and refine your ideas. It is possible to take good quality pictures using a digital camera with its automatic setting switched on. However, making use of manual settings will allow you to control exposure and aperture, giving you more opportunities to be creative with the camera and enabling you to develop your levels of understanding and photographic skill.

Important skills include:

- careful framing of your subject matter
- selective focusing
- controlled exposure
- For moving subjects, an effective shot can be taken by following the subject with the camera. Alternatively some cameras have a sports mode which increases shutter speed, whilst others have an action facility which takes a sequence of shots continually while the shutter button is pressed. Refer to your camera handbook for instructions.

In the **digital darkroom**, being selective in the use of tools is important. Adobe Photoshop will enable you to make an image more crisp, add depth and tonal values.

Adobe Photoshop will enable you to make an image more crisp, add depth to tonal values, focus attention on areas by adjusting their sharpness, edit unwanted elements, adjust colour ranges and values, and crop or reframe an image to improve composition. As in wet process photography, demonstrate control over tone and colour balance, composition and focus.

Remember

'Undo history' is a very useful means of returning to earlier stages in your processing and also provides a means of logging your changes and decisions: use a screen grab to highlight and save the history pane which can then be printed off and incorporated into your preparatory work.

AQA Examiner's tip

Use screen grabs of the history pane as evidence of the processes used with your photo editing software.

Key terms

Digital darkroom: a term often applied to the processing of digital images on a computer using one of the wide range of software programs available.

Case study 22

Developing skills in Photography

In the recording of his subjects, Yousef demonstrates his understanding of formal elements. Images are carefully framed and focused, exposure is controlled and lighting effects create a dramatic mood (see Figure 2.38). Informed by his investigation of Friedlander's work, Figure 2.39 shows the car door mirror skilfully framed and focused to create an image where multiple viewpoints are brought together.

Positive decisions have been made to look for locations and artefacts with the potential to inform and suggest. Images of graffiti, gates, alleyways and signs all create a sense of the desolate urban landscape that he set out to portray in his initial brief. In Figure 2.40 good lighting and careful focus allied to skilful composition maintain clarity and balance in images that convey a strong sense of location and urban culture. Humour, desolation and despair are captured thoughtfully and with conviction. Without a strong understanding of the skills associated with controlling depth of field, shape relationships, light, shadow and, in close-up shots, texture, Yousef's work would lack the conviction and quality that it so clearly possesses.

Fig. 2.38 *Workbook*

Fig. 2.39 *Workbook page showing strong connections to contextual sources*

Fig. 2.40 *Images of graffiti*

In Figure 2.41, the workbook page demonstrates the thematic connection between two images in which the contrast is dramatic. In one, the padlocked doors are an impenetrable barrier, in the other the gates bar our way to a private leaf-strewn drive.

Figure 2.42 shows views of urban decay where abandoned possessions become the central interest, and the dramatic use of angled viewpoints contribute to their meaning. The basketball hoop and coat evoke a story, whilst the lack of sky in the other image creates a sense of claustrophobia. Again, Yousef's annotations support the images which were 'taken with the idea of loneliness in mind – the jumper left there had a strong sense of abandonment and seemed to have a story behind it', and he states that he wants to create a sense of 'the emptiness inspired by Baltz'. The settee in Figure 2.43 further demonstrates his awareness of selecting different viewpoints to shift meaning, whilst the witty juxtaposition alongside the one-way sign adds to his ideas.

Fig. 2.41 *Photography workbook page*

Fig. 2.42 *Photographs: urban decay and abandoned possessions*

Fig. 2.43 *Workbook page*

AQA Examiner's tip

Generate and explore potential lines of enquiry through different processes and media.

Key terms

Hue: a distinct colour of the spectrum; pure colour without the addition of black or white.

Saturation: depth or intensity of colour.

■ Using media and techniques to review and refine ideas as they develop

Experimentation with media, materials, processes and techniques can have a profound effect on the development of your work and you can dramatically alter the appearance and qualities of an image or object by exploiting the characteristics of a particular material or process. Ideas can be generated, developed and refined by meaningful, focused experimentation with different media and techniques.

■ Experiment with the size and scale of your studies.

■ Review and refine composition, layout or design.

■ Experiment with the relationship between shapes or forms, and their relationship with the framing edge or surrounding space.

■ Change the technique from a precise, cleanly outlined drawing or cutting method to a looser or torn technique.

■ Experiment with brushes that are different shapes and sizes and with different thicknesses of paint, fabric, wire, etc.

■ Shift the tonal contrast from hard to soft or vice versa.

■ Alter the balance between positive and negative shapes.

■ Change the **hue** or **saturation** by scanning your image and manipulating it on a computer.

■ Make a small 3D maquette and then draw or photograph it.

■ Refine your handling and control of the medium.

Fig. 2.44 *Dionne Barber keeps a wide selection of brushes close at hand*

Case study 23

Reviewing and refining ideas in Textile Design

As already described in case studies 15 and 17, Alex's study sheets for her A2 externally set assignment show her approach to the use of textiles media and to the learning objectives set out at the beginning of this chapter. In your work you should aim to address all of the objectives in an integrated or holistic fashion. Figure 2.45 shows how ideas from contemporary designers are analysed alongside the possibilities which Alex sees in her own photographs, prints and drawings.

The sheet of studies linking to Mersh's Mercury Dress of 2005 shows how the architectural structures of The Eye could be developed using wooden supports, and these are subsequently tied into McQueen's shoulder fan concepts (1998) in Figure 2.46. Alex's own photographs of her sample print designs displayed on a mannequin and her associated collages provide a clear example of how translating ideas across media and using different working methods can be fruitful: she is able to quickly visualise what her final piece might look like.

Fig. 2.45 *Research sheet: ideas and possibilities*

The sequence of study sheets also contains some subtle elaborations on colour and juxtapositions of materials through layering and construction techniques. For example, in Figure 2.47 a combination of enhanced photographs, washed drawings, glued threads and machined samples show the development and refinement of Alex's ideas. Also, in Figure 2.48 a selection of different samples has been presented which show how layering of mesh and printed surfaces, ruffles, channel pleats and dowels could work together in the final design. The considered use of closely related colours in the 'threads' interpretation from one photograph of The Eye creates a harmonious effect which is taken forward to the final design.

Fig. 2.46 *Study sheet: McQueen's inspiration and development studies*

This sculpted tulle dress was created by Hussein Chalayan for his before minus now collection (spring/summer 2000). I find it positively screams "structure" to me. Chalayan continuously finds inspiration from architecture, in this case "blob" architecture. Blob architecture is an attempt to rob the viewer of any particular viewpoint or clear perspective, creating a system of architecture that has no clear front or back. Hussein Chalayan has followed this principle to create his ruffled tulle dress; though when it is seen on a body one can trace the outline of the bust and the waist, if this garment where to be removed it would indeed become a "blob" – without shape or purpose. Hussein Chalayan does not design conventionally according to the code of fashion.

I like the idea of incorporating ruffles into my samples and designs, to create blocks of "blobs". My images of the Eye are very structured and and I would like to create areas of contrast between highly structured and lines, and more indefinable areas. However, if I include 3D str such as dowelling, to these sections then I too will create a garmen contours and conventions.

The sample to the right was an attempt to vary between ruffles and plates by sewing straight lines but pinching the fabric into place underneath. Some of the chiffons within were first pleated using shibori, but I think that the entire effect is not as clear cut as I would wish, as seen in the photographed ign idea above.

Fig. 2.47 *Study sheet showing the development and refinement of ideas*

Monoprinted lines overlaid onto dragged paint samples on paper and fabric allow Alex to preview possible effects for the final surface treatment of the fabric. Some of these are collaged into fashion design drawings which are evaluated (Figure 2.49): 'I find this best helps me to visualise how the design would appear if it were actually created. The shoulder decoration I fear, would be overpowering, but I like the continuation of pleats down ... I attempted to recreate a spiked necklace inspired by ... McQueen's fan and ... Mersh's ruff. However by trying to incorporate all of the other aspects of my sampling as well I find this design is too full, and falls ... short of my intentions'.

Fig. 2.48 *Study sheet*

Fig. 2.49 *Study sheet*

In her final piece, produced in the 15-hour period of supervised time, Alex has made selective use of her ideas and resources. All the fabric, including the ruffles was screen printed, and she has made use of 'scratching and dragging paint ... and machine embroidery' as these relate to [her] monoprints and photographs. Pleats and folds were created in the various layers of fabric before it is constructed as a dress.

Remember

A study may show not only observation skills, but may also make connections to a contextual source or provide evidence of developing ideas.

The architectural feel of her chosen contextual material is successfully incorporated into the final outcome which has an asymmetrical waist line, complemented by a triangle of ruffles and a dowelling structure to the skirt. Figure 2.51, showing the front view of the dress, demonstrates how the embellished fabric is used around the figure to create a dynamic yet balanced fashion item.

Fig. 2.50 *Final design sheet*

Fig. 2.51 *Final outcome: front view of dress*

Fig. 2.52 *Close-up of dress showing printed, stitched, torn, cut and pleated fabric*

Case study 24

An artist's approach to reviewing and refining ideas in Fine Art

'I work on a number of paintings at once to keep myself and my work fresh and energised. Creating traces of people and places and my own physical presence; using palette knives, my hands and fingers, rags and turps to sculpt the paint on the canvas.'

Dionne resources her ideas from fieldwork where she makes sketches and takes lots of digital photographs. She then works through her ideas, experimenting, researching, selecting and rejecting. She reflects on exhibitions she has visited and places that hold significance for her. Dionne likes the immediacy and directness of drawing with a pen and also with oil bars which are a solid form of oil paint that produce rich textures and colour.

Photographs are taken at each stage and the work is continually reviewed and analysed. If it has been overworked then with reference to a photograph it can be taken back to an earlier stage. She looks at the photographs away from the canvas, sometimes asking others for advice.

Fig. 2.53 *Sketches used to review and refine work*

Fig. 2.54 *Dionne Barber painting*

Key terms

Aesthetic qualities: the characteristics or visual aspects of an image or artefact which we regard as beautiful or which provide pleasure to our senses.

Refining ideas – looking closely

The detailed study of a subject can give rise to an interest in surface texture or patterning which could inspire a fabric design or ideas for ceramic forms and their surface decoration. Figure 2.55 illustrates the exploration of pattern and design possibilities developed from the investigation of playing-card designs.

The close scrutiny of a theme or subject through the camera may lead you to an innovative and personal discovery of **aesthetic qualities** in unexpected places. For example, the litter or debris in a city street becomes a dramatic pattern of light and shade in the low-angle light of late afternoon (see case study 25 on Photography).

Remember

For close-up work good lighting is essential to keep the whole subject in focus: there can be depth of field problems, so use a tripod which will allow you to use a slow shutter speed and smaller aperture.

AQA Examiner's tip

Review and refine your work systematically during its development.

Fig. 2.55 *Examples of design studies*

Fig. 2.56 *Workbook for case study 25: the urban scene*

Reviewing and refining ideas using digital processing of images

Earlier in this chapter some key techniques were outlined for the control of images in recording with the camera. The following are other methods and techniques that you might use when developing and refining your work.

■ Combining images is one of the many powerful techniques available to you when working with software such as Adobe Photoshop: in effect you are able to create a **photomontage** by selecting, cutting and pasting or erasing various parts of images and then combining them as in Figure 2.58. (See also case study 26.)

■ Another method might be to use the **opacity** setting on various layers in a digital image to reveal underlying patterns and shapes, creating a more three-dimensional feeling to a design.

■ Distortion filters, if used selectively, provide you with the opportunity to manipulate an image to resemble expressionist or abstract styles of painting. Case study 20 provides a good example of the use of Cinema4D to enhance the design of playing cards.

■ Texture effects can be employed to add a feeling of an image being produced on canvas, watercolour papers or even everyday surfaces such as stone or brickwork. Again, use these selectively, creatively and with understanding.

■ The printers and the papers that you use to print your images are the final link in the digital image chain. Demonstrate, in the choices and settings that you select, that you have control of the medium and understand the potential of the equipment you have available.

Key terms

Photomontage: a collection of photographic images combined together in the same scene or frame.

Opacity: how dense an image appears – less opacity means that the image appears transparent or see-through.

AQA✓ Examiner's tip

Choice of paper is part of the selection and use of materials process: sometimes a print on plain paper will suffice for a reference image, but it is important that final outcomes are printed to the best quality that you can manage.

■ Remember

When printing look carefully at the end product. Are the colours and tones what you want? Is the image to the right scale for your subject?

Fig. 2.57 *Using Adobe Photoshop to manipulate images*

💡 Case study 25

Using media and techniques to refine ideas in Photography

In this exploration of his local environment Yousef has pursued a detailed and thorough investigation of the streets of Manchester using digital and traditional darkroom photography. Rather than focusing simply on architectural detail, he has been inspired to look for ideas and images which relate to his brief and the contextual sources that he has researched. Some images are informed by the work of Friedlander and Baltz, whilst others concentrate upon issues of composition and the narrative potential of selected subjects. His annotations reveal critical understanding at each stage of the development of his images. For example:

- 'I wanted to cram as much urban landscape as I could into a narrow tight space … to represent how crowded cities can get'.
- 'I wanted to use the scaffolding as a grim frame'.
- 'Inspired by Aidan O'Rourke … I increased the contrast … to make the lines stand out and guide the eye'.
- 'The subtle contrast … adds a slight "noir" feeling to the image … I had in mind how Baltz took photos of walls but also how Friedlander would get quite close to his subjects'.

Fig. 2.59 *Workbook: the Urbis building in Manchester*

Fig. 2.58 *'Before' and 'after' images demonstrating enhancements to a digital image*

Yousef has produced a collection of related images in which he shows technical skill in his use of the camera and in his manipulation of Adobe Photoshop, as we see in Figure 2.59 where he has made a montage of two images of the Urbis building. Figure 2.58 also demonstrates the refinements possible through digital processing. Although well composed, the first image appears grey and rather flat. By using brightness and contrast enhancements Yousef has given the image more depth and our attention is drawn to the foreground textures of the cone and brickwork. All of his final photographs represent a personal view. They successfully realise his intentions and clearly demonstrate understanding of his chosen sources and subject matter.

Case study 26

Using media and techniques to refine ideas in Graphic Communication

Esperant's study sheets show how he has refined his ideas. For example, Cinema4D is used to give a three-dimensional character to the design motifs which, at an earlier stage, were flat. Final designs areproduced for both surfaces of playing cards and in Figures 2.60 and 2.61, the application of the design across suits is identified, analysed and refined.

In his development studies the reverse sides of playing cards are given equal attention to those designs for the fronts of the cards. Esperant has used collage, drawings in ink and pencil, splashed and washed inks and paint to create images which have been scanned and layered using Adobe Photoshop. In some studies he has recognised that the designs have become too cluttered and has adjusted the colour, texture and tonal balance to address this. He has also explored a wide range of possible variations through digital processing which has required careful manipulation, organisation and reorganisation of motifs in multiple layers. Figures 2.62 and 2.63 also illustrate the clear generation and progression of ideas through to the final designs shown in Figure 2.64.

Fig. 2.60 *Study sheet: obverse designs*

Fig. 2.61 *Design ideas for the fronts of playing cards*

Fig. 2.62 *Further design ideas*

Fig. 2.63 *Resolved designs*

Fig. 2.64 *Final playing-card design*

Your use of resources to develop ideas in Art and Design is linked to your skills and understanding of media and materials. A clear understanding of the characteristics of media may be gained through experimentation and sustained practical experience with materials to help you to develop your skills. The success of your work depends upon your developing a working familiarity with media and materials and the confidence with which you apply this knowledge and understanding.

Having read this chapter you should now be able to:

- develop your knowledge and understanding of media, materials, techniques and processes

- select and explore appropriate resources, media and materials to develop ideas and intentions

- explore the characteristics of media

- develop skills in handling media and techniques

- use media and techniques to review and refine your work.

3 Recording ideas and reflecting on work and progress

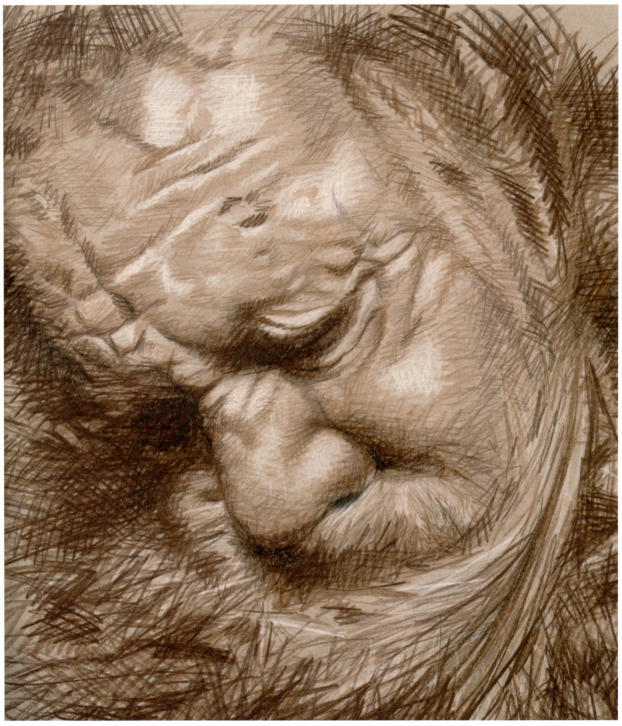

Fig. 3.1 *Study in brown chalk*

■ Recording ideas

Recording visually

In making studies in response to starting points and source material you will record your ideas, observations and insights. It is what you do in making your first sketches, drawings, thumbnails, jottings or notes when exploring your initial ideas or in making your first responses to your source material. It is also what you do when you collect information through sustained, **analytical studies** that record your observations from close study of your source material. **Recording** shows the ways in which you have thought your way around ideas and solved problems. You will record your observations, your thinking and the decisions that you make as you develop ideas, as you explore contextual material and as you analyse and respond to your sources. As your work on a project moves forward, recording ideas and observations should enable you to demonstrate clearly the journey you have made in developing your ideas.

💡 Case study 27

An artist recording ideas in Textile Design

Louise Watson is a textiles artist specialising in embroidery. She exhibits three times a year with the Gloucestershire Guild of Craftsmen and throughout the year all over the UK.

Louise describes her sketchbooks as her resource of images that can be used to provide source material for ideas. She adds material all the time. The sketchbooks are where initial recordings and thoughts are moved around, modified, added to, developed and reviewed. Louise combines small delicate studies of pebbles with experiments in stitch derived from them.

Louise explores ideas and experiments with different techniques and combinations of media, using memory and imagination to create her own personal response. Her immediate environment in her garden provides much information. She records from direct observation much of the time, using pencil, crayon and watercolour. She finds mixed media collage particularly suitable for developing ideas for embroidery. A piece of work that Louise has recently finished is called *Footpath*. It is influenced by her studies of pebbles. Different threads and fragments of fabric have been embroidered into the main structure of the piece.

In this chapter you will learn how to:

- record ideas visually, in written and other forms
- record from direct observation and secondary sources
- use sketchbooks, journals and logs for recording and reflection
- develop critical skills to reflect on work and progress
- use digital media for recording observations and ideas.

■ Link

For more ideas on recording observations and insights in response to contextual material, see Chapter 1.

■ Key terms

Analytical studies: studies that analyse source material in depth.

Recording: the process of collecting information in visual, written and other forms and providing evidence of your ideas, observations and insights.

■ Remember

It is important to select appropriate media, techniques and processes for recording to be effective.

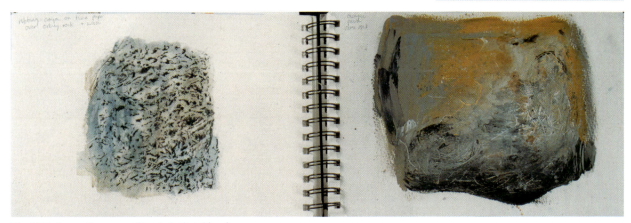

Fig. 3.2 *A page from one of Louise's sketchbooks*

Key terms

Evaluating: looking back, reflecting on the strengths and weaknesses of an idea or image, comparing ideas and images and making a judgement or decision.

Link

For more information about Louise's work, see www.brunelbroderers.co.uk.

AQA Examiner's tip

When appropriate, use a range of methods for recording ideas and intentions.

Remember

Recording your ideas, observations and insights should show the 'creative journey' in your work.

Recording ideas is the way in which you demonstrate and communicate your thinking. It enables you to stand back from your work and reflect on the directions it might take by having your initial ideas in front of you. Making a record of your ideas means that you can put yourself in control when it comes to **evaluating** and comparing alternatives and choosing the best line of enquiry. Rather than dealing with vaguely and partially formed ideas in your head, it makes sense to deal with them where you can see them.

Recording makes it possible to show the story or journey of your investigation and the development of your ideas. It will provide evidence of alternatives that you might have considered, the ways in which a direction has emerged and become established, and ways in which you have refined your ideas.

Fig. 3.3 *A detail of Louise's textile piece* Footpath

Fig. 3.4 *A page from one of Louise's sketchbooks*

■ Link

For more information about Art Deco and other design movements see:

- ■ www.vam.ac.uk
- ■ The Design Encyclopedia: Byars, The Design Museum of Modern Art, New York.

💡 **Case study 28**

Recording ideas in Three-Dimensional Design

In recording his observations and ideas, Carl shows his understanding of ways in which geometrical shapes and lines can create a sense of rhythm. He has used colour to suggest the different planes and levels in his ideas, a useful technique when anticipating their development in three dimensions. Carl has recorded the development of his ideas on A3 size study sheets.

Carl considered an idea based on Art Deco furniture design, but gradually he focused on the characteristic shapes and forms found in automobile design of the 1930's. In the five-hour period of supervised time, he chose to use clay as the medium in which to explore his ideas in three dimensions.

Fig. 3.5 *Carl's ceramic piece*

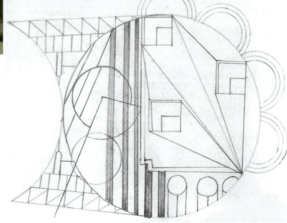

Fig. 3.6 *Carl's final design*

Your initial responses to a starting point, a theme or a design brief, might be recorded in a series of sketches, drawings, thumbnails, design roughs or photographs in which you identify and explore possible avenues of investigation. This kind of visual thinking could enable you to generate initial ideas and to identify what source material you will need for your research. It could also help you to explore more than one starting point as well as possible angles or slants on the topic you choose.

Experimentation with materials, processes and techniques could also be a way of generating ideas, and studies such as these might themselves form a record of your initial thoughts.

Links

- See Chapter 1 for more about developing ideas.
- See Chapter 2 for ideas about experimenting with materials, processes and techniques.

Fig. 3.7 *Experimental studies in wax resist*   **Fig. 3.8** *Contemporary fashion and corset ideas*

Fig. 3.9 *Recording ideas*

Key terms

Storyboard: a series of drawings that show ideas as a sequence of frames or scenes for film, video or motion graphics, or a sequence of photo images that tells a visual story or narrative.

Maquettes: small 3D studies or models that explore shape, form and space, often translated from drawings. A maquette is like a 3D working drawing.

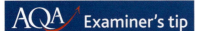

Examiner's tip

Make certain that your preparatory studies provide a visual record of how your ideas have been developed.

Link

See case studies 1, 3, 5 and 6 in Chapter 1.

A record of the developing ideas could be in the form of compositional roughs, studies, thumbnail sketches, design sheets or working drawings in which you show the exploration and refinement of your ideas, compositions or designs. Providing evidence of compositional alternatives, alternative colourways, refinements of colour and tone will record the ways in which your ideas are developed and gradually refined. **Storyboards** can be a record of exploring and developing ideas for film or video sequences. Contact prints can show a series or sequence of images that demonstrate the development of ideas in photography. Test strips, test prints and layout roughs can provide a record of the refinement of your ideas. In 3D work, ideas can be recorded visually in working drawings, **maquettes** and models.

Case study 29

Recording ideas in Art, Craft and Design

Becky is an AS student who has responded to a theme of 'The body in question'. An A3 sketchbook contains the early recording, contextual resource and later exploratory work using mixed media. Sculptural maquettes developing the idea of body sculpture and corsets were presented life size together with a number of larger drawings. From the outset Becky wanted to explore a range of media and ideas but needed to find sources that would suggest a line of enquiry. The work of Lorraine Shemesh, who has explored the idea of distortion through figures in water, informed the investigation and development of Becky's ideas in which she was able to see the possibilities for fluidity, abstraction and bold use of colour.

Fig. 3.10 *Lorraine Shemesh, Echo – 2005, 64 x 66 inches, oil on canvas, Courtesy Allan Stone Gallery, NYC*

Becky photographed a series of carefully composed images of a friend in a swimming pool using a basic underwater camera and a compact digital camera.

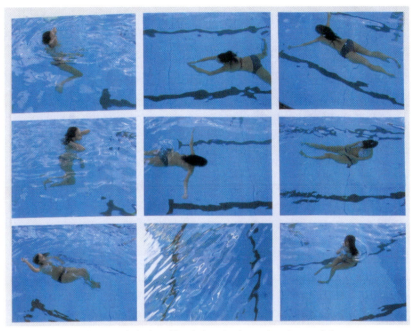

Fig. 3.11 *A page from Becky's sketchbook showing her swimming pool shots*

Fig. 3.12 *Three studies in oil pastel and acrylic by Becky*

Links

- See Chapter 2 for ideas about selecting resources and experimenting with materials.
- See Chapter 1 for ideas about using contextual.
- For more information about David Hockney's 'Pools' see www.artchive.com.

Key terms

Drypoint: a printmaking method in which a soft metal plate is engraved with a steel point then inked and printed.

Remember

You can record your observations, insights and ideas in different ways.

She took photos of a pool with the sunlight creating patterns on the surface of the water. With the results likely to be unpredictable, a large number of shots were taken from different angles and viewpoints. Becky was particularly interested in the linear patterns that were created and looked for other examples of paintings of swimmers. She saw links with David Hockney's early swimming pool pictures. Further shoots were undertaken as the topic developed and Becky's ideas were refined and modified.

Using the photos as source material Becky began to experiment with pen and wash, oil pastel, acrylic paint and wax resist to suggest movement and distortion, trying new ways of using the media to see what effects might result. In this way she began to develop a personal visual language. In these pictures Becky built up the pastel and paint in layers allowing the colour underneath to come through in places.

She used the immediacy and directness of **drypoint** to produce a series of prints.

Recording in other forms

Recording observations and insights will be evident in your practical work in a variety of ways, but it can also be in various other forms.

You might record insights in discussion about your work with your art teacher or with your group of students. You might support your work with an oral presentation where you explain aspects such as your response to your source material, the development of your ideas or the ways in which contextual material has informed the development of your work.

Your observations might be recorded on audio tape, on video, using PowerPoint or in the form of a digital sketchbook. You might choose to make brief notes to help you plan your work and in photography, graphics or ceramics, for example, you might wish to annotate images to record technical data, or details of processes or techniques.

Reflecting

Ideas and their development need thought and the specification encourages you to think and to reflect in depth. **Reflecting** on issues, themes or starting points, delving into your own experiences of places you have been to, things you have seen, heard or read, could point you towards source material and help you to shape your ideas. Developing the ability to reflect will help you to get a feel for situations and for atmosphere, a location, a sense of place, and it will enable you to identify and select possible directions for your investigation. You will need to develop the ability to look back and reflect on your work and its progress and also to reflect on contextual material.

Key terms

Reflecting: thinking, evaluating, comparing, looking back on progress, considering ideas, your response and directions within the work.

Link

For more ideas on reflection in art you could look at: Gerhard Richter, *The Daily Practice of Painting* Thames & Hudson, 1995.

Recording from direct observation and secondary sources

In your work, recording observations and insights will be evident in a number of ways. You might experiment with media, processes and techniques and at the same time, in the same studies, be recording observations from your source material. For example, you could be experimenting with biro and correction fluid, or drawing ink and white acrylic paint, working from your source material of a natural object or an environment.

Recording from observation, whether from **first-hand sources** or from **secondary sources**, could include your initial responses to your source material in loose, rapidly worked sketches and drawings to get the feel of the subject matter, to identify its characteristics, its potential and the problems it offers. It will also include recording observations and insights from sustained, analytical studies in which you study your source material in more depth.

Recording from direct observation

The advantage of working from direct observation of first-hand or primary sources is that you actually experience the source material. You can touch it, feel it, even smell it, so that you are able to use all of your senses to develop your understanding and knowledge of it. You will be more aware of its scale, texture, colour and subtleties of tone, and, if the source material is a place such as an urban or natural landscape or an interior, you will be more aware of its atmosphere.

Fig. 3.13 *Recording in Photography: Providence © Iain Stewart*

Key terms

First-hand sources: source material that you can see and study from direct, first-hand experience. For example, studying a painting in a gallery, working from the landscape or from textured surfaces.

Secondary sources: source material that you experience through reproductions or images produced by someone else.

Link

See Chapter 2 for ideas about media, processes and techniques.

Link

For more information about Iain Stewart's work see:

- www.iainstewartphotos.co.uk
- www.nationalgalleries.org.

In recording his observations and ideas with the camera (see Figures 1.36, 1.65, 3.13 and 3.15), Iain Stewart, a professional photographer, puts a great deal of effort into identifying appropriate locations for his work. He often works in remote places and chooses to photograph extremes of weather and light conditions. His beautifully observed and reflective images are highly expressive of atmosphere and place.

In recording from direct observation you might choose to draw directly from natural or manufactured objects or environments, artefacts, buildings or structures that are around you or in a gallery or museum. You might, for example, choose to investigate the human figure or animals through a series of observational studies. You could use traditional media such as pen and ink, pencil, chalk and paint, but you could draw in other media such as wire, wax, stitch and clay and you can use a camera or computer to record your own images and observations.

■ The Photography student will record observations from first-hand experience directly through the lens, using a traditional camera, digital media, film or video.

■ In Graphic Communication, the student might use a camera to record observations and collect source material, drawing from direct observation in developing ideas for illustration, or in recording observations through the direct experience of selecting and manipulating typography.

■ A Textile Design student might record observations from natural objects, the landscape or direct from the experience of experimenting with and manipulating media.

Link

See Chapter 2 for ideas about experimenting with media, techniques and processes.

Remember

There are many different ways in which we can draw.

AQA Examiner's tip

Working from first-hand sources enables you to experience the source material and use all of your senses.

Fig. 3.14 *Detail of bodice form in plaster*

Direct contact with contextual material also has advantages. Studying a painting, sculpture, print or installation first hand should give you the opportunity to look closely at the handling of media and to reflect on the work's scale. Although reproductions in books or on websites often show the dimensions of work, it is difficult to visualise the impact without actually seeing it. It is much easier to appreciate the way in which paint has been manipulated, the ways in which brush strokes have been used, and to experience the quality and nature of colour if you can see the work in front of you. The experience of being able to explore a sculpture from all angles will be more meaningful and a more intense experience than seeing it reproduced on a flat page. By actually seeing the object, your insights into elements such as scale, mass, volume and form could be sharper and more vivid.

Link

See Chapter 1 for ideas about ways in which contextual material can inform the development of your ideas.

Fig. 3.15 *Recording observations and ideas: © Iain Stewart*

Links

- See Chapter 1 for more ideas on contextual material.
- See Chapter 2 for more ideas on experimenting with media.

Link

For more information on the work of Lucian Freud see:

- www.artchive.com
- www.tate.org.uk
- www.artnet.com.

Remember

Media react differently to different paper surfaces.

Fig. 3.16
Self portrait. *Lucian Freud, 1985*

Case study 30

Recording from direct observation in Fine Art

Jordan had worked from the human figure during part of his AS course and decided to return to the theme for his personal investigation. He chose to develop his work from his own photographs and drawings of an old man. Most of the studies in which he recorded his observations of the figure range from A5 and A4 to A2. The final piece is A1, acrylic on canvas. Jordan has been particularly influenced by the drawings of Rubens, Michelangelo, Degas and especially the paintings of Lucian Freud.

Jordan began recording from direct observation and from his photographs of the posed figure using a range of media and techniques. There is evidence of reflection and sympathetic use of media and handling when trying to resolve difficulties and problems associated with viewpoints. Soft pencil, fineliner and pen and ink are used in rapid initial studies while acrylic paint and pastel are used in more detailed work to produce sustained and penetrating images. Different surfaces and materials are used.

Jordan's recording of his observations and insights ranged from loose, initial sketches and drawings to sustained analytical studies in which he increasingly focused on the idea of characterisation and developing the expressiveness of his work.

■ **Did you know?**

Jordan worked on a variety of surfaces that included cartridge paper, newspaper, sugar paper, Ingres paper, hessian and canvas.

Fig. 3.17 *Conté crayon on brown wrapping paper*

Fig. 3.18 *Study in chalk on newspaper*

Recording from secondary sources

Secondary sources can take various forms and they can be a valuable resource in the development of ideas. Images that you might find in magazines, newspapers or the internet could provide you with material that you need, or with something unexpected that starts you off on a line of thinking and the beginnings of an idea. Secondary sources in the form of images, sound recording or video could, for example, increase your awareness and understanding of an issue that you are engaging with in your work.

Although seeing works first-hand is ideal, contextual material in the form of reproductions in books, exhibition catalogues, magazines, CDs and the internet, are fantastic resources that give you opportunities to record your observations and insights from material that otherwise you might not see.

Your investigations might identify exciting images that have potential for you to use and to respond to in developing your own ideas. The images might provide a springboard for you to demonstrate and exploit your creativity and imagination if you respond to them through sustained investigation, experimentation and development.

If you choose to make use of secondary sources, be selective and discriminate between what is appropriate to your intentions and what is not. Work that is made in response to secondary sources should show evidence of reflection and analysis in the same way as that developed from primary sources.

AQA Examiner's tip

Use your critical judgement and understanding in choosing your source material and selecting from it.

■ Remember

Use your source material creatively.

■ Link

See Chapter 1 for more ideas about using contextual material.

Fig. 3.19 *Lorraine Shemesh, Echo – 2005, 64 x 66 inches, oil on canvas, Courtesy Allan Stone Gallery, NYC*

Fig. 3.20 *Drypoint print and pen and ink studies*

Case study 31

Recording ideas using secondary sources in Three-Dimensional Design

During his AS course Carl has been developing ideas and skills that have resulted in three-dimensional outcomes. He had explored possibilities with fired clay and wanted to use the techniques he had learnt in his externally assessed assignment. He responded to a question encouraging students to look at vessels for holding liquids or dried materials which could be either decorative or purely functional. Carl chose to research the Art Deco movement which seemed to him to offer a number of possibilities for using strong geometrical shapes.

Carl first looked at the background to Art Deco and its application to architecture and product design. In particular he began to analyse the forms to be found in furniture and automobile design. Books and the internet were used as sources and Carl made annotations to support and inform his visual material. Carl recorded and refined his ideas in compositional roughs and thumbnails based on his research. Both visual work and annotations show his ability to reflect on his work and progress, and how his ideas were reviewed and refined. Carl was aware that his designs needed to be suitable for translating into clay with the opportunities, restrictions and characteristics that the medium presents.

Remember

- In analysing and investigating contextual material you will often have to use secondary sources in the form of gallery postcards, reproductions that have been photocopied in colour or scanned from books, or the internet.

- Galleries and museums are excellent resources but usually do not allow photography.

Did you know?

Some images resourced from the internet and gallery websites are small files and do not print well.

Link

For more information on Art Deco see www.lepoix.de.

Fig. 3.21 *One of Carl's initial source sheets*

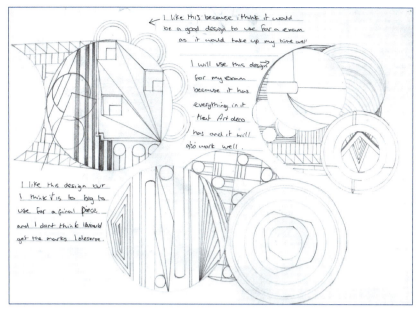

Fig. 3.22 *One of Carl's initial recording sheets*

The importance of drawing

Drawing can be in a wide range of different media and in making drawings you can have a wide range of intentions and purposes which include:

- recording your initial observations or ideas
- recording events, situations and locations
- exploring different drawing materials and techniques
- sustained, searching, close observation and analysis
- exploring problems and resolving them
- as a means of communicating ideas and insights.

Through drawing you can develop your understanding of media, techniques and processes, and you can develop your observational abilities and skills. It is through drawing that you can expand your awareness and make genuine discoveries about the visible world by looking not just at the outside of things, but trying to get an understanding of their underlying structure and meaning. Drawing can help you to look hard and to see the unexpected. It can develop your perception and stimulate your inquisitiveness. It can be exciting both as a process and as a highly expressive medium.

There is a huge range of fine art and graphic media that can be used for drawing, but artists and students, especially in experimental studies, also use non-art materials.

Drawing is a broad concept that is not limited to making marks on paper. The photographer who has a strong understanding of **formal elements** can effectively draw through the lens of the camera by being highly selective in manipulating line, shape, form, tone and texture. The textile designer can draw in stitch, carefully and sensitively tracing the path of lines and manipulating the sewing machine as a drawing tool. The sculptor might choose to draw in wire or clay and the graphic designer can draw directly onto the computer screen using a mouse or stylus pad. Drawings can be made by manipulating an element such as 'line' in ways

Links

- See Chapter 2 for ideas exploring the characteristics of media.
- See Chapter 2 for ideas about experimenting with materials.

AQA Examiner's tip

Be aware of the different purposes of drawing.

Did you know?

- There are many techniques and materials that you can use to draw with.
- Drawing can have a range of different intentions and purposes.
- Drawing can be evident in your work in different ways.

Key terms

Formal elements: often called visual elements – line, shape, colour, tone, form, mass, volume, space, texture, composition. The language or vocabulary of Art and Design that we use to make images and objects.

Fig. 3.23 *A portrait study in chalk pastel*

Fig. 3.24 *Chalk study in brown, black and white*

that include using light, by controlling drips and runs in liquid media, by using stems, reeds, sticks or twigs, or by making folds or cracks. Drawing can be in the form of incised lines in lino, card, or an etching plate or Perspex, or on the ground, in mud, sand or snow.

Drawing with clay

Peter Voulkos's work is direct, immediate and has an uncompromising urgency about it. Slabs and wedges of clay are loosely attached to one another while blocks and ridges are punctuated by slits and cracks. Voulkos is literally drawing in space with the clay. His pieces suggest conflict and aggression symbolising the terrible forces of nature.

Fig. 3.25 *Drypoint print and pen and ink studies*

Fig. 3.26 *Schoppleinstudio.com, Source: Courtesy of the Voulkos & Co. Catalogue Project www.voulkos.com*

Drawing in stitch

Audrey Walker is a textile artist who studied Fine Art at Edinburgh College of Art and at The Slade School of Art. Regarding figure drawing as an essential part of her work, she has accumulated a large collection of figure studies which inform and stimulate her ideas. In her work she has explored elements of mystery, uncertainty and anonymity.

Audrey found the possibilities of merging her fine art studies with the alternative tradition of embroidery and the building of surfaces with threads and fabrics to be liberating, and her teaching career culminated in heading the Department of Embroidery at Goldsmith's College. In *Gaze 1V*, Figure 3.27, the **picture plane** is alive with energy. The delicate combination of hand and machine embroidery reflects her early drawing experience and it has a **translucent** quality that is both haunting and penetrating. Complex colour combinations are achieved by the interaction between threads that fuse together to express form.

◼ **Link**

For more ideas on different forms of drawing, see the work of the artists Andy Goldworthy: www.andygoldsworthy.com www.goldsworthy.cc.gla.ac.uk and Richard Long: www.richardlong.org.

◼ **Key terms**

Picture plane: plane of the physical surface of a painting or image.

Translucent: ink or paint which allows some light to pass through it.

■ Link

For more information about Audrey Walker's work see: www.embroidersguild.com.

■ Remember

Drawing can be used to:

- ■ Observe
- ■ Analyse
- ■ Plan
- ■ Speculate
- ■ Develop ideas
- ■ Release intentions
- ■ Explore formal elements
- ■ Communicate.

Fig. 3.27 *Audrey Walker,* Gaze 1V, *1999*

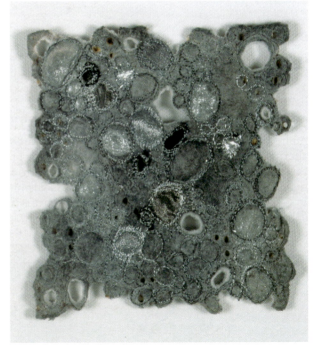

Fig. 3.28 *Louise Watson, drawing in stitch*

Using sketchbooks, workbooks and logs for recording and reflection

In this specification, you can present your work in any appropriate form. Preparatory work and supporting studies can be presented entirely on study sheets or as mounts of studies. You can also choose to use a sketchbook or workbook for all or some of your studies.

Sketchbooks and workbooks

Sketchbooks and workbooks can be in various forms, but do not confuse the function of a sketchbook with a scrapbook. As part of your investigation and development of ideas you might need to collect materials and images. These should be selected and assembled with a sense of purpose and be appropriate to what you are planning to do. The sketchbook could include initial responses to your source material, sketches, drawings, colour notes, contextual material, experimental studies and development work. You might prefer to use a sketchbook for only part of your project, especially if you want to explore working on a larger scale or on various different scales and surfaces.

> ■ **Did you know?**
>
> Sketchbooks and workbooks can be in many different forms.

💡 Case study 32

Using a sketchbook for recording and reflection in Art, Craft and Design

Becky chose to record images in an A2-size sketchbook. She collected photographs, made studies, referred to the work of others and explored ideas. She felt that organising her work in this way helped her to focus and see when and where there might be gaps in the development process. Becky avoided packing the book with a collection of irrelevant material and every page helped her to reflect on the progress of her work.

Fig. 3.29 *Examples of recording. Lorraine Shemesh,* Echo – 2005, 64 x 66 inches, *oil on canvas, Courtesy Allan Stone Gallery, NYC*

Fig. 3.30 *Photographs used for recording Becky's sketchbook*

Journals

A **journal** usually includes information and notes about technical or other aspects of Art and Design relevant to your area of study. It might, for instance, include notes on the materials, techniques and processes in printmaking, ceramics, textiles or photography. It could include observations and your reflections on contextual materials that are relevant to your work and provide examples. A journal is usually ongoing and long term, perhaps being added to and developed over a whole year of study.

Logs

A **log** will be focused on specific tasks or events such as gallery or museum visits, site visits, workshops, relevant work experience and courses, and will provide a record of your observations and personal reflections. It could also include material such as technical information, notes and a photographic record of the activity or event. For example, you might make a detailed record of a course or workshop on commercial screenprinting, or you might record a week's work experience working on a live project brief in a graphics studio.

💡 Case study 33

An artist using a sketchbook for recording and reflection in Textile Design

Louise Watson keeps a sketchbook for recording ideas for her textile work. She describes it as 'her storehouse of images ready to be used at any time'. Whereas Becky used her book for collecting images and exploring ideas and techniques on a relatively large scale, Louise prefers a smaller book that she can slip into a pocket or a bag so that it is always there, ready for her to make notes and visual recordings. Her books are full of intimate studies and jottings that provide her with material to work from. She records her ideas and observations in a variety of media and is keen to see what happens when chance is allowed to play a part.

Fig. 3.31 *Louise's studies of rust*

Fig. 3.32 *Recording in a variety of media*

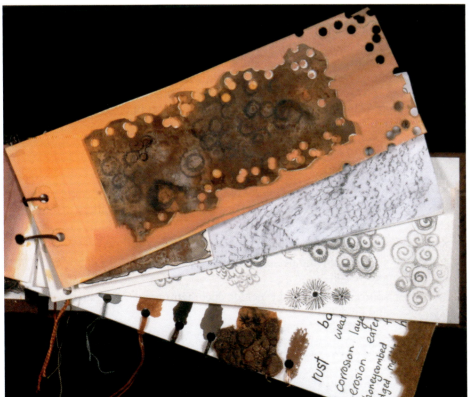

Fig. 3.33 *Recording observations from rock forms*

Remember

- Do not copy from your sources.
- Use your own words.
- Acknowledge the sources of quotations.
- Record the sources of art, craft or design work referred to, documenting artist, title, date and any additional information you think is relevant, like medium and dimensions.
- Record in a bibliography the author, title and date (if known) of any book, article, website, video or recording that you have used.

Developing recording skills for the written elements

In written work, recording your observations and insights needs the development of skills that will enable you to identify and select information and material, and to use specialist terms accurately. Sources of information can be visual, oral, in written form, in sound recordings and in video. Whether you are writing a written reflection or a personal study, plan your investigation and develop a set of objectives, key points or questions to give shape to it.

Recording

In written work where it is appropriate you should record:

- information that you have obtained from sources that could include books, articles and reviews, exhibition catalogues, gallery materials, the internet, interviews
- the views, ideas and interpretations of other authors
- your critical and personal response to relevant works of art, craft and design
- sources, which might include documenting relevant gallery visits and fieldwork.

In recording your observations and insights, aim to have a clear idea of what you are looking for and be purposeful and well focused in looking and in making your notes. You might be recording your observations about a work in which you are exploring:

■ the subject, theme, issue or idea

■ aspects of formal elements: line, tone, form, mass, volume, space, colour, texture, composition, design or layout

■ aspects of media, processes and techniques.

Developing critical skills to reflect on work and progress

Developing critical skills should enable you to reflect on your work and its progress and enable you to make informed decisions and judgements. In the journey of developing ideas in a project, you will make a lot of decisions. Some will be relatively easy and straightforward and others will require a good deal of thought. For example, you will exercise critical skill in using your knowledge and experience of media and techniques to make decisions about what is the most appropriate medium to use in response to a particular source to achieve the outcome that you want. Reflecting on your work and progress, you will look at it critically, evaluating what you have done and making comparisons between studies, different media and techniques.

Responding critically to the work of others, developing your ability to analyse and reflect on their work will help you to form opinions and preferences of your own.

You can demonstrate critical skills by:

■ using with understanding and insight a visual vocabulary of formal elements in practical work

■ selecting and using appropriate media and techniques

■ analysing source material with intention and purpose

■ selecting, using and responding to contextual material so that it informs the development of ideas

■ relating one image to another

■ using a critical, specialist vocabulary with appropriateness and accuracy

■ reflecting on work and progress, demonstrating evaluation and decision making and providing evidence of the **creative journey**

■ selecting source material and identifying its potential.

💡 Case study 34

Developing critical skills in Art, Craft and Design

Becky pursued a line of enquiry that focused on the textural marks and effects achieved by Degas, in particular looking at his pictures of women drying themselves after bathing. She posed a model and, informed by Degas's drawings, made studies of her own, using oil pastel. This helped her understanding of Degas's technique.

She also studied the draped figurative work of Tamara de Lempicka. As a result of looking at the work of these two artists, drawing from

Remember

To reflect on your work as your ideas develop and as you experiment with and explore media, materials, techniques and processes.

Key terms

Creative journey: the complete journey of your work from investigation to the development of ideas and the realisation of your intentions.

Links

■ For more information about analytical and critical understanding see Chapter 1.

■ For more information about Edgar Degas see www. artcyclopedia.com.

Link

For more information about the artist Tamara de Lemicka see:

■ www.tragsnart.co.uk

■ www.arthistoryarchive.com.

Link

For more information about the textiles of Pauline Burbridge see:

■ paulineburbridge-quilts.com.

Links

■ See Chapter 1 for ideas about using contextual material.

■ See Chapter 2 for ideas about experimenting with media.

direct observation and another series of her own photographs, Becky began to see potential in the sculptural possibilities offered by the draped torso. She also became increasingly aware of the textile work of Pauline Burbridge and produced a series of experimental squares using a wax resist technique.

From this point Becky increasingly began to focus on the possibilities of stitch and mixed media used in a three-dimensional way to create body sculpture. Strong linear, rhythmic images, based on studies derived from her photographs of swimming pools, were constructed from fabric, cardboard, paint and reflective material. These evolved into moulded body forms. Further experiments using acrylic paint gave ideas about colour and texture. The breadth of her initial recording of ideas enabled Becky to reflect on a range of possibilities. The bodice was moulded over a body form in plaster and bandage, and the bold linear pattern was built up on the surface. A combination of paint finishes and varnish has produced a translucent effect of water.

The body form in papier mâché and glued and stitched fabric developed the idea of distorted forms in water. The body forms make interesting connections with Becky's original photos of figures in water and there are also references to corsets and fashion illustrations.

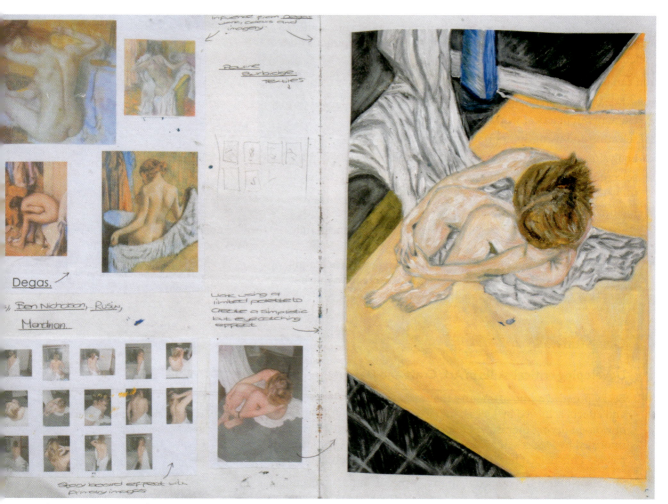

Fig. 3.34 *A study in oil pastel*

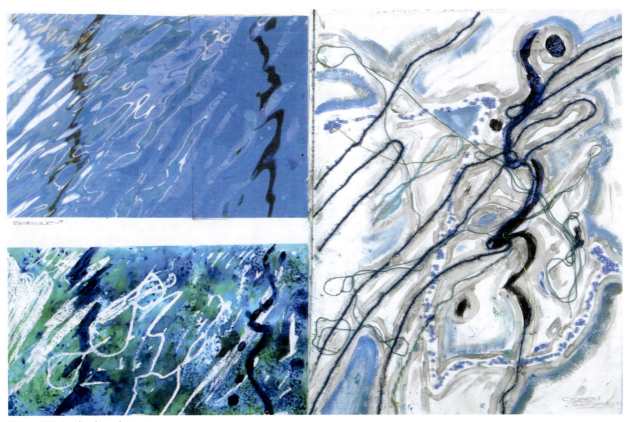

Fig. 3.35 *Studies based on water*

Fig. 3.36 *Study from water*

Fig. 3.37 *Bodice form in papier mâché and fabric*

Case study 35

An artist developing critical skills in Textile Design

The development of ideas is always at the heart of Louise's creative activity. She has to find out how far it is possible to take an idea. Experimenting with techniques and materials she is keen to exploit creative accidents and new visual and tactile effects. Her mind is always posing questions. By training her mind to work in this way, she is looking for alternatives and is always open to the unexpected.

Louise's exhibition group meets regularly to view each other's artwork and make positive criticism. In this environment, exchanges of ideas give a fresh perspective on work and provide an additional stimulus for ideas. Discussions can also help to resolve design problems and suggest new starting points. 'Working on your own is limiting', she says, 'vocalisation often defines what we are doing. Makes you think!' Louise uses a digital camera to record images of colour, texture or shape, which are added to her sketchbook. Sometimes she makes drawings from these images to develop her ideas or to explore possible starting points. Figure 3.39 shows the *Footpath* piece in its entirety and Figure 3.40 is a study of rock that uses paint scratched into it to create texture. Louise has developed a visual language that is appropriate to her work and she analyses her source material with a sense of purpose, always looking for potential for her ideas.

> ■ **Remember**
>
> Experimental work can often produce accidental marks or effects that can stimulate ideas.

> ■ **Did you know?**
>
> Sometimes you can create the conditions for creative accidents to happen.

> ■ **Remember**
>
> Discussion with your art teacher and with other students can help you to clarify your ideas and intentions.

Fig. 3.38 *Recording the effects of rust*

Fig. 3.39 Louise Watson: footpath

Fig. 3.40 *A study of a rock form*

Link

For more ideas about critical understanding see Chapter 1.

Did you know?

- You can demonstrate critical skill in making connections between one image and another.
- You can demonstrate your understanding of visual vocabulary in both practical and written elements of the work.

Case study 36

Developing critical skills in Fine Art

Jordan's ideas show insight and perception in the way that development takes place in articulate, expressive work. He has worked into the studies, working and reworking passages of the drawings, recording his observations in depth without sacrificing vitality. The process of building up the drawings is evident, creating networks of lines and laying in tonal values to express form. The initial marks retain their freshness even when they develop into a more complex image.

Jordan has shown critical skill in selecting and using appropriate media and techniques, in reflecting on his work and in the decisions he has made. He has used a visual vocabulary with understanding and insight and has exercised critical skill in analysing source material and in making meaningful connections between one study and another.

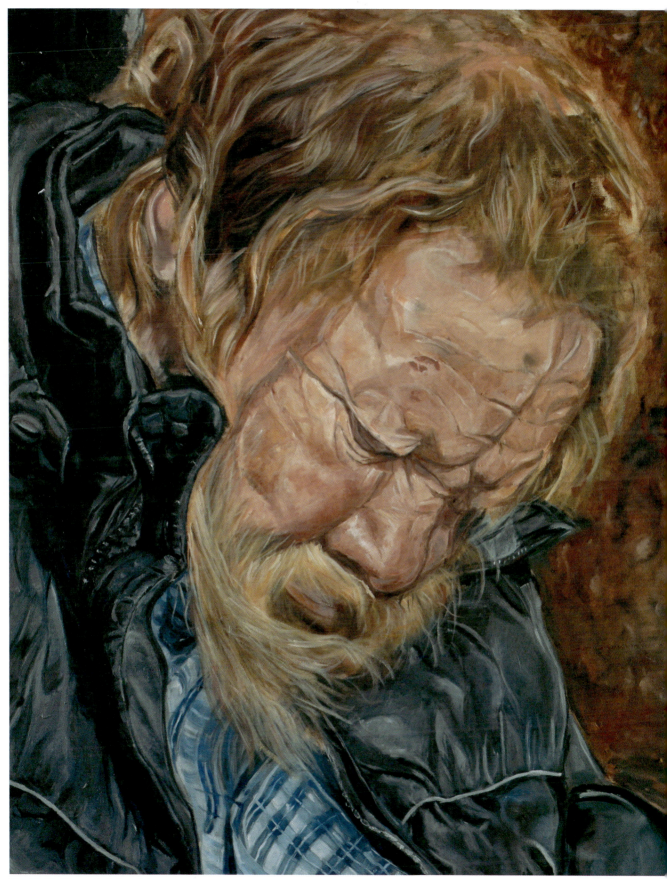

Fig. 3.41 *Figure study in paint*

Fig. 3.42 *Painting: acrylic on canvas*

Using digital media for recording

Digital media are used extensively in Art and Design, particularly in Graphic Communication and Photography, and also in Textile Design and Three-Dimensional Design and in Fine Art. Digital photography is most often used, as a medium for recording from source material, as a sketchbook tool for the fine artist, and as a creative medium for both Photography and Graphic Communication students. Caligari Truespace and Macromedia Flash are used in animation and PowerPoint is sometimes used to present preparatory work in animation, motion graphics and light-based media. ICT is used in all areas of study in Art and Design to resource and reproduce contextual materials, for presentation and, where appropriate, word processing.

Computer software is being used more skilfully and students are becoming more independent, selective and creative in how they use programs such as Adobe Photoshop and CorelDraw. Graphic Communication students use digital media to manipulate images, typography and layout and to record the process of their investigation, experimentation and development of ideas. Photography students increasingly use software to manipulate and process images.

Textile Design students use digital media to develop their ideas, often using it to manipulate colour, tone, texture, pattern and to explore alternative colourways. Three-Dimensional Design students use software to produce visuals and, especially in product design, it is used to develop ideas and to record the development process. Where digital media are used by students, decisions made in developing ideas are increasingly recorded by contact prints and screen grabs that document the exploration and manipulation of images and design elements.

Having read this chapter you should now be able to:

- record in visual and other forms your ideas, observations and insights
- select and record from primary and secondary material related to the chosen starting point
- record and reflect in sketchbooks, workbooks, journals, logs or on mounted sheets
- demonstrate critical skills in reflecting on your work and progress
- use digital media for recording.

Link

For more about digital media see Chapter 1 and Chapter 2.

Did you know?

Digital media are valuable resources for:

- Recording ideas and observations
- Developing ideas
- Documenting your work
- Resourcing contextual materials
- Processing and presenting work.

Link

For more ideas about digital media for recording see the case studies:

- Chapter 1 – Case study 3 and 7
- Chapter 2 – Case study 19, 20, 26, and pages 89 and 103
- Chapter 4 – Case study 37, 39 and 43.

4 Making a personal, informed and meaningful response

Fig. 4.1 *My red balloon*

In exploring and developing ideas, you have the opportunity to make a creative response in a way that is personal to you. Your work will be informed by knowledge and experience from exploring ideas, experimenting with materials, developing skills and from looking at the work of other artists, craftspeople and designers.

As your work makes progress in the course of a project and from one project to another, you will develop a personal, visual language to express your ideas. You will use visual elements and media in ways that have a quality and character that is your own.

A personal response

Your personal response is the way that you interpret, react and respond to ideas and your source material through your work. It is personal to you because it is the result of your own investigation and you are expressing your own ideas and insights. We see things and express our own ideas differently, using our imagination in a creative and uniquely personal way. This is one of the exciting aspects of art, craft and design.

Fig. 4.2 *A close up of Simon Ryder's 'Pochard': his personal expression of a birdsong*

An informed response

In order to make an informed response you will develop your understanding, knowledge and awareness of materials:

- by experimenting with media, processes and techniques
- by looking at the work of others
- by developing your observational and manipulative skills
- by developing your understanding of formal, visual elements.

Sustained investigation and reflection on your ideas will enable you to explore **lines of enquiry** in greater depth, and this will inform the development of your personal response.

Looking at appropriate works by other artists, craftspeople or designers should help you to develop your own personal, visual language and to develop an informed personal response. It can contribute to your

In this chapter you will learn how to:

- develop a personal, visual language
- respond to ideas, issues or themes critically
- realise intentions
- make connections between different aspects of the work
- present practical and written work.

Key terms

Lines of enquiry: the direction you take and your lines of thinking, in investigating sources and ideas, in experimenting with media and in developing your ideas.

Link

- See Chapter 1 for more about investigating and developing ideas.
- See Chapter 2 for more about experimenting with media, techniques and processes.

understanding of **image making**, composition, **process** and techniques, but it can also give you insights into ways of responding to ideas and developing them in a personal way. In selecting contextual material, think carefully about those aspects which are most appropriate to your work.

Decision making is an important aspect of developing an informed response because the choices and decisions you make will enable you to express ideas and develop a personal, visual language. Exploring media, developing skills and analysing the work of others should help you to make sound, informed decisions in your own work.

Fig. 4.3 *Mixed media study sheet*

A meaningful response

For your response to be meaningful, develop clear intentions in the investigation and development of your ideas and in your response to the theme, idea or issue you have chosen. Sustaining an investigation and thinking or reflecting on your work will help you to develop your ideas in a meaningful way. Aim to study your work in depth.

Your investigation and the development of your ideas should be undertaken with a sense of purpose and a spirit of enquiry. Be inquisitive. Ask questions of your source material, your work and of yourself. Make the most of opportunities to engage creativity with ideas and materials, and be serious about your work.

■ Developing a personal, visual language

All of the case studies in this book and in the online resource connected with it show ways in which artists and students have each developed their own, personal language in response to ideas and materials. The personal nature of this language is an important aspect of Art and Design. Whatever area of study you work in and whichever media you use, the subject is about expressing and communicating ideas creatively and imaginatively, in ways that are personal to you.

Your work will develop a character as individual as your personality, your handwriting or signature. It will change and develop as you change and develop and as the way that you see and understand things alters with experience and time. The characteristics of your work will develop during this course of study. They may develop during the course of a project or in response to an idea, a theme or an issue that you investigate.

A personal language is not something that you can suddenly acquire. It should develop as you identify the characteristics of your source material and respond to them in developing ideas, exploring contextual material, as you experiment with media, record observations and realise your intentions. It will grow as you gain knowledge and understanding of visual elements, materials and techniques, as you gain awareness and insight by manipulating your visual elements, and as you develop skills.

AQA Examiner's tip

In written work, support your personal response with direct references to the work or text.

■ Remember

- ■ Art & Design is about communicating ideas, observations, feelings and information.
- ■ Developing a personal visual language will enable you to realise your intentions.

 ## Case study 37

Developing a personal visual language in Photography

Ben has produced a well-researched project exploring illusion. Annotations have helped to identify lines of enquiry and to make connections with the work of others. Through experimentation Ben has been able to create the visual effects he wanted and has made a very individual personal response. He has chosen to present his ideas in workbooks, with development prints and **10 × 8** outcomes mounted on board.

Ben chose to experiment with different ways of recording, exploring botanical and mechanical forms as his themes. He took close-ups of exotic flowers using a conventional SLR camera and a macro setting. Other photographs were taken with a compact digital camera, and image editing software was used to enhance highlights. Experimenting with different compositions, angles and depth of field, Ben developed a collection of images of plant forms that display their sculptural qualities and strong colour.

Also, he explored similar qualities in mechanical objects, in close-ups of shiny, brightly coloured steel forms. They began to take on a personal identity of their own as Ben investigated scale, depth of field and colour.

Experimenting in this way, exploring his source material, the medium and techniques, Ben developed a personal, visual language to express his ideas.

Key terms

10 × 8: a standard size of photographic paper, measured in inches.

Fig. 4.4 *One of Ben's initial plant studies*

Fig. 4.5 *Investigating mechanical forms*

Case study 38

An artist's personal visual language in Fine Art

Simon Ryder is a professional artist who trained as a zoologist before studying Fine Art at the Royal College of Art. He has been Artist in Residence at the Wildfowl and Wetlands Trust and at Gloucester Cathedral. Currently he is working as Artist in Residence at the National Wetlands Centre, Llanelli and at the Nuclear Medicine Department of the Gloucester Royal Hospital. Simon is a founder member of artNucleus, an artist's organisation that focuses on art in response to locations.

Simon's methods of working mean that throughout the process of developing ideas, his intentions change. He describes this as 'a shifting field that has to be negotiated'. Often he has to work with constraints that influence the final realisation. These include time, access to the location or, sometimes, finding the right person, as Simon likes to collaborate with scientists and other artists. Collaboration enables him to discover new techniques and technologies, as he did with Dr Smith of the British Antarctic Survey, a software developer researching speech recognition in birdsong.

Figures 4.6 and 4.7 come from a project called 'Birds of the Antarctic'. Simon never decides beforehand what a project is about. He says '*Finding out* what it is about is the project itself'. In this case he began with the idea that he wanted to work with sound in some way. He took photos, made sound recordings and videos and collected any other material that he found interesting.

Figure 4.6 shows a computer projection of the bird call of a Pochard. It is possible to take a sound and break it down into three parts: its moment in time, its frequency and its amplitude. From this information it is possible to create a computer-generated image which has the appearance of an abstract landscape.

Link

For more information about Simon's work and projects see www.artnucleus.org.

Did you know?

Simon's work demonstrates ways of using a range of media including photography, sound and video recording, digital and electronic media.

Fig. 4.6 *A computer projection of a Pochard bird call*

Fig. 4.7 *Simon, like many artists, started his project by making notes, which helped him to develop his own personal, visual language*

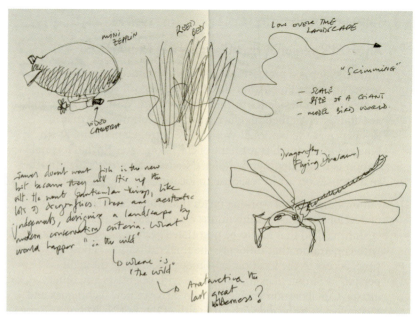

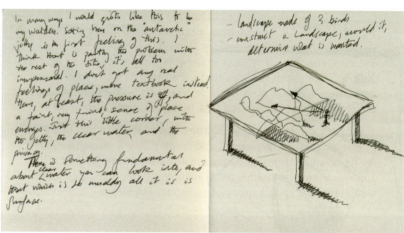

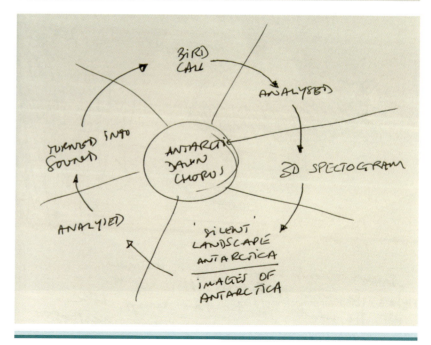

■ Responding to ideas, issues or themes critically

Responding to ideas, issues or themes critically means learning to make informed choices, connections and decisions in your work. It is about developing opinions and preferences. In demonstrating critical understanding, you are more likely to understand your chosen theme or idea in depth.

You should:

■ make informed choices and decisions in recording the development of your ideas, in experimenting with media and in realising your intentions

■ make informed connections with the work and ideas of other artists, designers, craftspeople and photographers

■ show your understanding of formal elements in responding to the work of others.

■ Aim to engage with starting points, ideas, issues or themes in depth, establishing a clear focus to your investigation.

■ Ask yourself questions about your idea, issue or theme.

■ Respond to ideas, issues or themes, starting points or design briefs with insight and understanding rather than taking things at face value; your research and investigation should be sustained and in depth.

■ Form opinions and preferences, responding critically.

■ Make informed decisions about the use of materials and techniques to develop a personal visual language.

■ Make connections with and be informed by contextual material in developing ideas.

■ Make connections between different aspects of your work.

■ Demonstrate critical understanding in discussing your work and the work of others.

■ Demonstrate awareness of creativity, originality, intuition and innovation in the development of ideas.

■ Plan and organise your investigation, demonstrating understanding of your chosen theme or idea so that you can develop your ideas in depth.

■ Show skill, accuracy and appropriateness in using specialist language.

Where you are required to make a written response, try not to take ideas at face value. When looking at and analysing the works of others, and when reading the ideas and insights of other authors, use your inquisitiveness to ask questions of what you look at, what you read and, of yourself.

■ Link

See Chapters 1, 2 and 3 for more about responding to ideas and demonstrating critical understanding.

AQA Examiner's tip

■ Learn to make informed choices, connections and discusions in developing your work.

■ Develop your understanding of ideas, materials and the work of others.

■ Remember

Intuition is an important element of creativity in Art and Design.

💡 Case study 39

An artist responding critically to ideas, issues or themes in Fine Art

At the start of each commission, Simon considers and reflects on the nature and character of the location and the environment where he is working. Walking into a bird hide at the Wetlands Trust, Arundel, immediately gave Simon his focus for that project.

'Originally, I came here with my sound-recording equipment expecting to make an acoustic artwork out of birdsong. In the hide I came across this quote from Sir Peter Scott: "Antarctica is … the last bastion of silence". My sound recordings started to become silent, to become pictures of the sounds I had recorded here at Arundel – the sounds themselves left to the imagination.'

Fig. 4.8 *Birds of the Antarctic:* 'Pochard' *(detail)*

Fig. 4.9 *Birds of the Antarctic: the* 'Pochard'

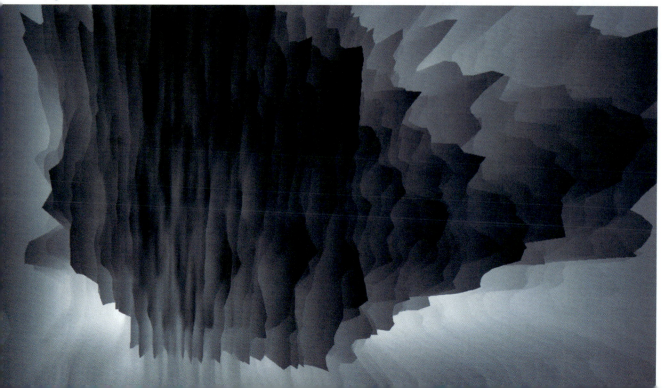

Using software normally used for speech recognition, Simon was able to transfer his sound recordings into shapes and generate a two-dimensional image created with inkjet print on canvas.

Simon's work is an example of how artists look at different issues and circumstances that they would like to make a statement about. Sound and digital media are integral elements in his work. He responds critically to ideas in having preferences and in making choices and connections between different aspects of his work.

Links

■ For more examples of the photography of Stephen Gill, see www.stephen-gill.co.uk.

■ For more examples of the photography of Andy Small, see www.andysmall.co.uk.

Case study 40

Responding critically to ideas, issues or themes in Photography

Scale and texture began to be more evident in Ben's work. Intense colour is important still, but movement and individual identity give his images a personal focus. Ben became increasingly aware of the creative possibilities of digital photography to combine images to create surreal effects. He also began to experiment with a colour replacement tool using a software program.

Ben discovered the work of photographers Stephen Gill and Andy Small who both create effects in their work by combining different elements of source material. Gill does not use digital manipulation but adds materials such as flower petals from the location to the surface of his photographs. He then rephotographs the work. One effect of this is to introduce an ambiguity of scale into the picture.

AQA Examiner's tip

■ Ensure that looking at the work of others is critical and meaningful.

■ Ask questions of your chosen idea, issue or theme.

■ Continue to ask questions as the work progresses.

■ Make informed choices, connections and decisions in your work.

■ Show your understanding of formal, visual elements in your work.

Fig. 4.10 *Stephen Gill:* Hackney flowers

Did you know?

I.M. Pei is just one of a number of influential late 20th-century architects whose buildings make dramatic statements in steel, concrete and glass. Richard Rogers, Norman Foster and Santiago Calatrava are three other architects who have transformed ideas about architectural shape, form and structure.

Links

- For more examples of I.M. Pei's work see www.greatbuildings.com.

- For more examples of Ian Simpson's work, see www.iansimpsonarchitects.com.

⚲ Case study 41

Responding critically to ideas in Three-Dimensional Design

For part of his personal investigation unit Andy decided to research the work of the architect I.M. Pei. He chose to analyse this influential 20th-century architect through written investigation and practical exploration.

By exploring written texts and examining photographs of his buildings, Andy has produced a piece of critical writing that looks into the personal style of the architect and his influence on contemporary architecture.

Andy explored, in the form of models, visual aspects of the structural forms of steel-framed buildings in Manchester and produced a number of 3D outcomes which reflect his investigations.

He photographed and made on-site notes about two buildings by the architect Ian Simpson, No. 1 Deansgate and Urbis in Manchester. Andy focused on the linear patterns created by the framework and the cladding panels in steel, concrete or glass.

Fig. 4.11 *I.M. Pei, Bank of China Tower*

Andy simplified these patterns and developed a series of linear images in 2D form that reflect his observations of the buildings. A sheet of studies in drypoint and mixed media explore diamond and related forms.

He looked closely at the exposed structural ribs on the interior of the pyramid structure which covers the entrance to The Louvre, in Paris. A number of drawings and prints investigate the triangular nature of this source.

No.1 Deansgate, MANCHESTER

Architect: Ian Simpson

Completed date: 2002

Type: residential

Material: steel framed superstructure

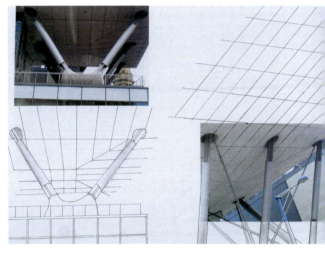

Fig. 4.12 *Ian Simpson, No. 1 Deansgate*

Fig. 4.13 *One of Andy's study sheets*

Fig. 4.14 *Pyramid du Louvre*

Link

For more examples of
Norman Foster's work, see
www.fosterandpartners.com.

Using a variety of materials such as strip wood, straws, cardboard,
paper and wire, Andy developed a range of 3D maquettes that
echo his building research and these gradually evolved into load-
bearing structures in their own right and became more complex.
He experimented with wire and card, drawing in three dimensions.
Structures made from straws explore construction methods based on
triangles and diamonds which add strength. More emphasis was placed
on the visual aspects of the bullet-shaped form which is informed by
the design of Sir Norman Foster's 'Gherkin' building in London.

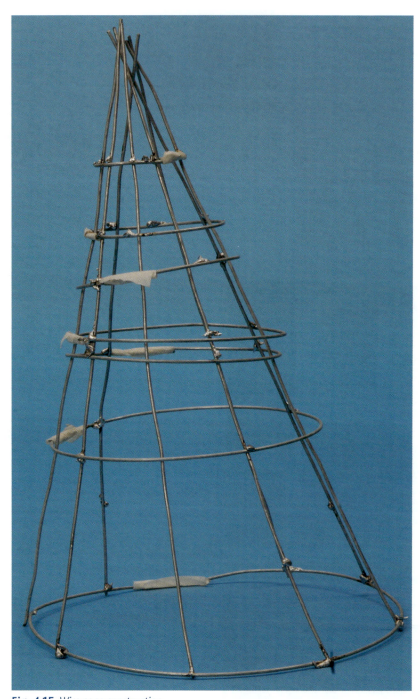

Fig. 4.15 *Wire cone construction*

Fig. 4.16 *Explorations in cardboard*

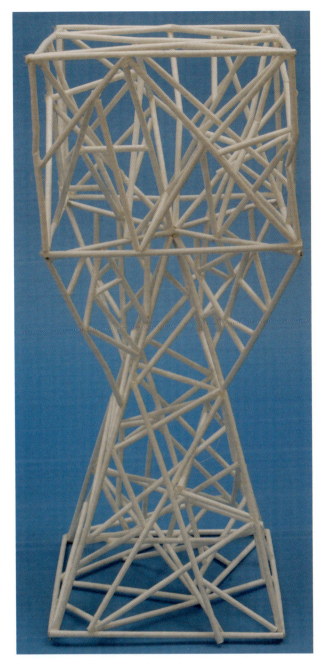

Fig. 4.17 *A large straw construction*

Fig. 4.18 *A cone-shaped straw construction*

■ Links

- ■ For more about critical understanding see Chapter 1.
- ■ For more ideas about selecting resources see Chapter 2.
- ■ For more ideas about drawing and recording see Chapter 3.

■ Links

- ■ For examples of Therese Oulton's paintings, see
  www.marlboroughfineart.com
  www.tate.org.uk
  www.artnet.com.
- ■ For more examples of David Bomberg's paintings, see
  www.tate.org.uk
  www.artcyclopedia.com.
- ■ For more examples of Peter Lanyon's paintings, see
  www.tate.org.uk
  www.artcyclopedia.com.

■ Did you know?

The development of Mathew's ideas was informed by the process and expressive handling of paint that he saw in the work of Thérèse Oulton, David Bomberg and Peter Lanyon.

♀ Case study 42

Responding critically to ideas in Fine Art

Matthew chose to look at the natural environment for his personal investigation unit. He worked in acrylic paint on canvas and the final outcome is in the form of two panels, each of which measures 120 cm × 84cm. Ideas were developed from fieldwork using his own photos of running water, stones and fallen wood in a small stream, making reference to a range of artists including Thérèse Oulton, David Bomberg and Peter Lanyon. The focus of the work developed as an investigation of rhythm, movement, line and solid form, and the ambiguity of looking down and across the field of vision.

A sustained, well-focused direction is established within the work and it gathers momentum in large-scale studies that explore and exploit the abstract potential of the source material. Matthew explored a fragment of an image, but this evolved into exploring two fragments or areas that would each stand up as complete, self-contained images but would also link together and across into two connecting panels.

In order to further his ideas, Matthew had to develop ways of using media to achieve an expressive, painterly response. Experimental studies used a range of media that included pen, marker, pastel and paint. Loose, quite aggressive lines express form, with crosshatching in pen to create shadow. Splashes of dilute colour help to give an impression of mystery, movement and a sensation of flowing water. In a charcoal study, the same viewpoint has been used but the handling of the medium gives a softer, less aggressive and more organic feel. Recording has been entirely visual though contextual material was acknowledged and documented. Source photos were taken on location and, from these, Matthew was able to identify and select material to develop his ideas.

Fig. 4.19 *Study in fineliner and watercolour*

Fig. 4.20 *Matthew: study in charcoal*

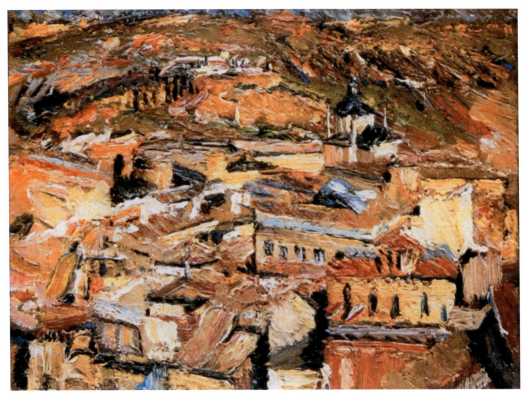

Fig. 4.21 *David Bomberg:* Outskirts of Toledo, *1929*

Fig. 4.22 *Sample of location photographs*

Matthew has demonstrated a critical response to ideas in the way that he has reflected on his work. He has exercised choice and made informed decisions in developing his work and in making connections between different images and between different aspects of the work.

Developing critical skills using written, spoken and visual means

If you choose to include annotations in your work and, in Unit 3 where a written response is required, all of your written or oral material should be grammatically accurate and its meaning should be clear. Where appropriate, spelling and punctuation should also be accurate and the text should be legible.

Both oral and written material should demonstrate critical skills and understanding in the use of specialist terms and critical vocabulary to analyse, compare and make meaningful connections between images and ideas. You might choose to support your work with an oral presentation using sound or sound and video, using audio tape recording, video recording, PowerPoint or CD.

In discussing your work or explaining it to others, you could demonstrate critical skills in explaining the development of your ideas and the journey of your work. You might focus on aspects that could include:

■ why and how you responded to the starting point
■ the decisions you made in obtaining and selecting source material
■ your aims and intentions
■ the decisions you made and the directions you explored
■ dilemmas and problems in your work as it developed
■ making connections between images, analysing and comparing them.

Fig. 4.23 *Source material from location work*

Fig. 4.24 *Study: acrylic on paper*

In practical work, develop your knowledge, understanding and awareness of specialist terms and visual and critical vocabulary. Learn how to use them in relation to your own work and the work of others. Use a critical vocabulary in making connections between works of art and in comparing one of your studies with another.

■ Key terms

Analytical drawing: a drawing that analyses source material in depth.

Working drawing: a drawing, to scale or full size, that shows the layout, plan, composition for a final piece or study.

■ Did you know?

Realising intentions can be achieved at different times during the progress of a project.

■ Realising intentions

You can realise your intentions at the conclusion of the project and at different times during the project. Realisation can take various forms and may have a single or several outcomes.

■ Because Unit 1 (the portfolio unit) can be made up of more than one project, a number of intentions may be realised.

■ In Unit 2 (the externally assessed assignment) your preparatory studies may lead to a fully realised piece or to further work of a developmental nature.

■ In the practical element of Unit 3 and in Unit 4 your preparatory work should lead to a finished piece or pieces that will realise intentions.

Finished pieces or outcomes can clearly be seen as intentions realised, but examples of other realisations could be in the form of an **analytical drawing**, a **working drawing**, a sheet of design ideas, a maquette, an exploration of stitching techniques, a photograph that is the culmination of a line of enquiry. In these, realisation could mark a point in your journey of investigation and in the development of your ideas.

Fig. 4.25 *Another close up of Ryder's 'Pochard', his original intentions of visualising birdsong have been realised*

Case study 43

Realising intentions in Photography

In order to understand more of Stephen Gill's technique, Ben took a series of pictures of a rubbish bin on its side on the pavement from very specific angles. On a photo he carefully laid out conkers with the smallest towards the back and the largest to the front. He then photographed the two elements together. Ben constructed another multiple shot using berries by the edge of the pavement to achieve a similar effect. A third photo shows a JCB tipping flower petals. In these images Ben has demonstrated understanding of his contextual sources and their appropriateness for the development of his own work. The outcomes show how he has used scale and the power of illusion.

Ben then began to look at work by Andy Small who photographs flowers in front of vibrant painted backgrounds. The images gave him more ideas about how to develop his interest in strong colours and the interaction of mechanical and botanical forms. Further development work included cutting and rearranging flower images on different backgrounds, again emphasising scale and contrasting subject matter.

A series of shots led to a complex series of digitally composed pictures with human figures grafted onto plant forms which alter the scale in the process.

Fig. 4.26 *Conkers on the pavement*

Fig. 4.27 *Berries on the pavement*

Fig. 4.28 *JCB and flowers*

Fig. 4.29 *Figure surrounded by leaves*

Fig. 4.30 *Poppy flower on text*

Fig. 4.31 *Figure emerging from flower*

Examiner's tip

Document any technical processes you have used.

A work book kept by Ben describes in detail how this was achieved by using a computer software program. He has kept detailed records and documented the whole process. An understanding of the use of positive and negative space was developed and particular attention was paid to the positioning of the hands and feet so that they connected in scale with the base image. Colour correction tools adjusted the weighting of images until the right balance was achieved.

Fig. 4.32 *A page from the workbook showing computer screen images*

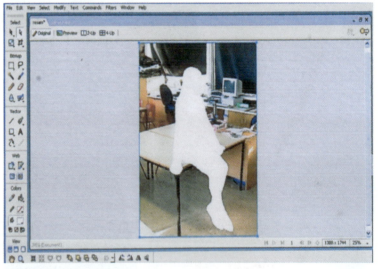

In this work, digital media have been used to create the effects that Ben wanted. The software has been used as a tool, just as a paintbrush or a sewing machine can be manipulated. Ben has made connections with contextual sources throughout the development of his work. By analysing techniques and using his critical skills Ben has been able to make informed choices and has used the information to develop his own ideas. The initial recording with its selection and attention to detail has informed development and further material has been found when he has needed it. By developing his own visual language and a critical awareness of his own work and that of others, Ben has been able to realise his intentions and present a highly personal and meaningful response.

AQA Examiner's tip

When using digital and electronic media, screengrabs can show the development of your ideas.

Fig. 4.33 *Another page from the workbook showing screen images*

Examiner's tip

Develop a clear focus to your work.

 Case study 44

Realising intentions in Three-Dimensional Design

In his personal investigation, Unit 3, Andy's written work explored aspects of I.M. Pei's work. Links are made to the work of Walter Gropius and Pei's attraction to sharp geometric designs. Andy is particularly attracted to Pei's design for the East Building of the National Gallery of Art in Washington, 1979. The site, sliced into two triangular spaces with a triangular atrium unifying the whole, gives a feeling of complexity and precision.

He says: 'I love the way new and old buildings (the pre-existing classical west wing) are functionally united and integrated by an underground tunnel animated by prismatic skylights.' Andy analysed the impact of Pei's other buildings such as the Bank of China Tower in Hong Kong, but he also looked closely at the structure that Pei is probably best known for, the glass pyramid ('Pyramid du Louvre') designed as an entrance to the Louvre Museum in Paris. In his writing Andy has focused on analysis of the modular system of triangles and tensioned rods that connect the whole structure. Experiments with strip material have added to the development of his ideas.

Andy's research has informed his practical work. His intentions have been realised in both written and visual forms and he has made appropriate connections between these different aspects of his work.

Fig. 4.34 *Experiments using wooden strips and straws*

Fig. 4.35 *Louvre Pyramid: looking in from the east corner. Source: www.GreatBuildings.com*

💡 Case study 45

Realising intentions in Fine Art

Matthew has realised his intentions in a mature and capable way. He has established a clear focus and clear intentions in aiming to explore and resolve complex issues. Although his painting is clearly abstract in nature, it is not too difficult to read and to decode its origins. We can recognise elements of the subject, though they are offered as clues that contain some degree of ambiguity and demand reflection from the spectator. The work is built up in acrylic but there are also linear elements where lines of oil pastel, Conté and chalk are drizzled onto the surface to enhance the expression of movement and water. Matthew's intentions have been realised throughout the project and, as his ideas develop, each study makes a strong contribution to the final outcome.

Fig. 4.36 *Study in acrylic*

Fig. 4.37 *Charcoal drawing*

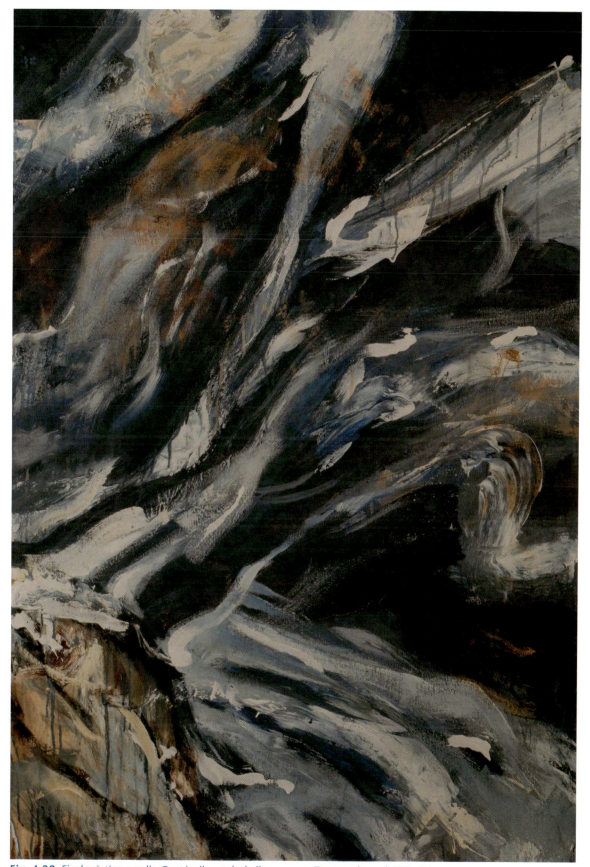

Fig. 4.38 *Final painting: acrylic, Conté, oil pastel, chalk on canvas. Two panels, each 120 x 84cm*

■ Making connections with different aspects of the work

Making connections with different aspects of your work is an important element in the investigation and development of your ideas and in the realisation of your intentions.

Critical understanding, the way that you form opinions, have preferences and make connections should enable you to make visual links and connections between different stages and between different aspects of your work. Your initial studies should suggest directions and possibilities for detailed analysis, the investigation of your source material and experimentation with different media, processes and techniques.

Connections can be made between:

■ source material, your ideas and realisation
■ the characteristics of different media, processes and techniques
■ realisations, and between realisations and developmental material
■ contextual material and the development of your own ideas
■ written and practical elements of your work.

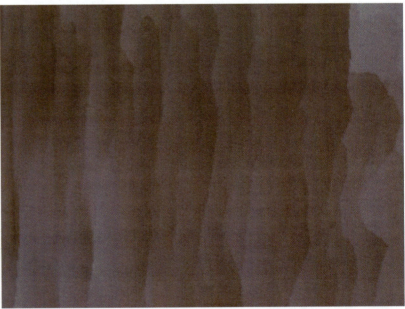

Fig. 4.39 *A work by Simon Ryder*

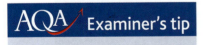

Written elements of your work can demonstrate and make clear the connections you have made between contextual sources and your own practical work and the ways in which contextual material has informed the development of your ideas. They can also make clear the connections between different aspects of your practical work, especially where the journey of your investigation and ideas may not be entirely obvious in a purely visual way.

You can also make connections between aspects of your work orally, in critical discussion with your group of fellow students or with your art teacher. You might have the opportunity to give a PowerPoint presentation or use sound and video to give a presentation in which you explain connections between the various elements of your work.

Case study 46

Making connections in Photography

Ben has brought together every aspect of his investigation, and the journey of the development of his work is very clear and easy to understand. Experiments with camera controls and subject matter were given impetus and direction by investigating contextual sources. Ben used them to inform the development of his ideas and to reflect on further directions he might take.

Fig. 4.40 *Figure lying on red flower-head*

💡 Case study 47

Making connections in Fine Art

Matthew's outcomes are expressive. All aspects of the work have been handled with confidence and there is a very clear, in-depth connection between the student and his chosen subject, the final image and what he is trying to do in a very painterly way. The final piece emerges logically and seamlessly from the preparatory work in which the investigation, development and final statement are cohesive and there is a strong sense of working in a **continuum**. Peter Lanyon's work such as *Lost Mine* and Thérèse Oulton's *Dissonance Quartet* and *Flare-up* inform Matthew's preoccupation with the paint surface, the construction of the image and the strong awareness of painterly process. Oulton is also the subject of Matthew's 3,000 word personal study.

The student has handled scale and the development process particularly well, showing perception and insight in continuing the process of development within the painting rather than simply enlarging and repeating directly from the preparatory work.

Fig. 4.41 *Peter Lanyon*, Lost Mine, *1959*

In his investigation into the work of Thérèse Oulton, Matthew made connections between the practical and written elements of his Personal Investigation.

In the written extracts he shows critical skill and understanding in analysing Oulton's work and in explaining the connection with his own work.

'I chose to study Oulton's work of the 1980s because of its expressiveness and exuberant gestural handling of paint: an abstract and emotional paint surface that never seems to become laboured or decorative, due to her impressive technical skill of composition, manipulation of light and application of paint. I find the painterliness of her work, its ambiguity and the quality of light in works such as *Dissonance Quartet* especially relevant to the development of my own work. It was for this reason that I chose to study her work of this period and not her most recent paintings.'

'I studied Oulton's painting, *Flare-up* in Leeds City Art Gallery. This large-scale work, over 2 metres and almost square, is predominantly red in colour. As we can see from the photographs I have taken, it has an intensity from the richness of its colour that contrasts with

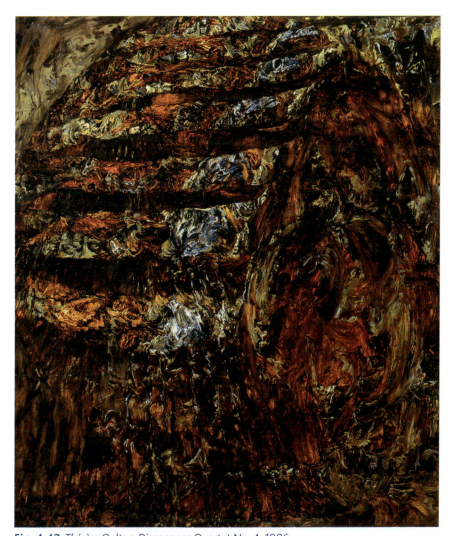

Fig. 4.42 *Thérèse Oulton, Dissonance Quartet No. 4, 1986*

the well-lit walls and clean lines of the gallery space. At first sight, the subtle light seems to be constructed from a limited palette of intense reds and browns. But looking closer, I found that the range of colour is more complex with yellow, yellow ochre, orange, greens, viridian and raw umber, especially in the vertical towards the right-hand framing edge and the thin yellow-gold line close to the left-hand vertical edge.'

'The painting contains great subtlety of colour and light. The surface of the paint has been combed through to create directional lines, not moving in one direction but converging, diverging, often changing in direction and intensity. These lines of paint seem to become finer, closer together and more restless as the light in the painting increases, broader and more calm as it lessens. The directional lines within the painting are predominantly vertical but a series of horizontal lines, like horizontal drips or score-marks, are pulled across the canvas. These connect with each other and seem to hover above the paint surface. As Andrew Renton[*] says, ... such marks suggest a possible direction that the compositional process might have taken.'

*Matthew's reference to one of his contextual sources.

In these extracts we can see that Matthew has become wholly involved in Oulton's construction of the painting and we can also see how her preoccupation with colour and mark-making has influenced his own practical work. The essay illustrates the value of first-hand study, when he makes his reponse to the work's scale, its presence in the gallery space and when he is analysing the detail of the paint surface.

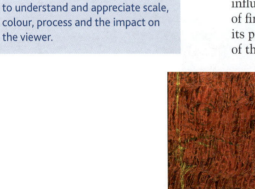

AQA Examiner's tip

First-hand experience can help you to understand and appreciate scale, colour, process and the impact on the viewer.

Fig. 4.43 *Thérèse Oulton,* Flare-up, *1992*

Fig. 4.44 *Matthew West: study for landscape, acrylic on canvas, 120cm x 84cm*

Presentation

Art and Design is a visual activity and the quality of its presentation should reflect the effort you have put into researching and developing your work.

Work can be presented in various ways; in the form of mounted sheets of studies, design sheets, sketchbooks, workbooks, logs or journals, files or CDs or well organised folders.

Take care with the layout of your studies on mounts and on pages in workbooks or files. Use your critical understanding and your ability to reflect to consider the relationship between one image and another. As far as you can, think about the sequence of your work and studies or images that you might group together. Balance size and scale, monochrome and colour, though the size of individual studies will often have some impact on what will go where. It is usually a good plan if, in mounting studies, you lay them all out first.

Presentation of Three-Dimensional work

Part of your presentation may be sculptural maquettes, structural or architectural models, packaging or fashion mock-ups, models, fired pots, tiles or test pieces. You might need to label work to make connections with studies or design sheets, and when presenting work in sculpture or ceramics consider taking photographs of the work in progress as well as the final piece. Fashion items can be photographed to show the work displayed on a model. Architectural models or site-specific sculpture or Three-Dimensional Design work could have photographs, illustrations or **visuals** made using computer software, showing how the work relates to its surroundings.

Fig. 4.45 *Examples of Ben's studies*

Presentation using electronic or digital media

If you are working in graphics, video, film and still photography you might choose to present your outcomes on CD or use a computer program such as PowerPoint. However, a PowerPoint presentation of final work must be supported with a 'digital sketchbook', a file, workbook or sketchbook, which shows the development of your ideas.

Being selective in presentation

In the Portfolio unit you may have a large volume of work that is distinct from your main project. For example, you might have produced a series of life drawings or a series of large prints that will not easily be presented in the form of mounts, a sketchbook or workbook. Be selective in your presentation of this work. Select sufficient for it to be representative of the work you have produced in the project, and present it in an appropriate way. Large work or study sheets could be presented in a well organised folio or folder.

Presentation is an important element of Graphic Communication and, like any other area of study, good work can be spoilt with poor, untidy presentation. Care and consideration should be given to the way in which each study relates to another, to the quality of presentation of captions and any hand-written notes. Designs for book and magazine covers, labelling and packaging designs, often benefit from mock-ups and from being photographed.

Photography students should give thought to the presentation of final images, particularly, whether a single image, a group or series. Photo images benefit from being grouped together selectively to show them at their best advantage, so that the viewer can easily make the connection between each image or, in a group or sequence see and 'read' images, individually and as a whole.

Fig. 4.46 *A mixed media study*

> **Key terms**
>
> **Font:** also spelt 'fount'; a set of type of one face or size; in ICT it is commonly used instead of 'typeface' to denote the style of type.
>
> **Typography:** the style and appearance of type for example, in print, an electronic page, a motion graphic, signage system or packaging design.

> **Did you know?**
>
> In photography, it is often difficult to distinguish between a contextual image and the candidate's own work. Acknowledging the sources of contextual material will make clear whose work it is.

Case study 48

An artist's presentation in different media for Fine Art

Simon Ryder feels that presentation is critical. He thinks his training as a sculptor greatly influences his approach to this aspect of the work. How the work is displayed is a vital ingredient in the mix. Everything is considered with the viewer in mind, including situation, lighting, framing, as well as exhibition invitations, the catalogue, signage and publicity. The overall look must be effective, enabling the viewer to fully experience the work. With his work *The Pochard*, Simon wanted the final image to be larger than the viewer so that the viewer had a relationship to the picture with his or her whole body, not just in the mind. It was important that the image had texture since computer-generated images are, by their nature, textureless, so the image was printed on canvas which has its own texture. The result is not the smooth, glass-like surface that we are accustomed to seeing in images created with electronic media.

Fig. 4.47 *The artist standing beside his work*

This is an interesting aspect of Simon's work and one that is clearly very important to him. It is the whole experience that needs attention and it illustrates to us the value of presenting artwork well.

Presentation of written material

Think about how to present annotations that you might choose to include if you think they are helpful. They could be in the form of jottings noted on site, an aide-mémoire for a drawing or photograph, details of technical processes or reflections on your own work or that of others.

Consideration should be given to the presentation of the required written element in Unit 3, the Personal Investigation, whether it is in the form of a written reflection on the practical work or a more formal personal study alongside the practical project.

The written reflection can be presented in any appropriate form, such as a report or journal or as a series of statements that are included as part of the practical project. It could be presented alongside appropriate images in a sketchbook or workbook, on mounted sheets of studies or in the form of a PowerPoint presentation. The work should be thoughtfully presented, whether it is word processed or hand-written. The work should take the form of extended writing, rather than annotation or notes.

The personal study can be presented in book form, in any appropriate size and format, or it could be in a more imaginative format, the nature of which might relate to its content. You might explore the opportunity to relate its visual presentation much more closely and imaginatively to the practical project. Care needs to be taken over the selection and presentation of visual materials that help to develop and illustrate ideas discussed in the text, such as photographs, reproductions, drawings, colour studies, plans and diagrams. Take care also, in selecting an appropriate font and in giving careful consideration to the relationship between text and images.

However you choose to present the written element of your work, its layout should be visually attractive, with good page layouts, well-chosen fonts and good-quality illustrations. Consider spacing, captions, headings and margins. Make sure that the text is legible and free from errors.

Link

See Chapters 1 and 3 for more ideas and information about written elements.

Remember

Remember to make your written work visually attractive and legible. Art and Design is a visual subject where presentation is important.

AQA Examiner's tip

■ Use the best-quality illustrations that you can get, such as reproductions from books or exhibition catalogues photocopied or scanned, gallery postcards or your own photographs. Images obtained from websites are sometimes too small or the resolution is too low.

■ Mount illustrations in a way that they will not become detached.

■ Acknowledge the sources of illustrations.

Having read this chapter you should now be able to:

■ present a personal, informed and meaningful response

■ use media and techniques to develop a personal visual language

■ develop critical skills using written, spoken and visual means in response to ideas, issues or themes

■ fully realise your intentions in practical and written elements of the work

■ make connections between different aspects of your work

■ present your work to show the journey of your investigation and the development of your ideas.

Case study references

Students

Alex: Case studies 15, 18, 23
Endorsement: Textile Design
Area of study: Fashion
Theme: Objects; Pattern and decoration

Andy: Case studies 41, 44
Endorsement: Three-Dimensional Design
Area of study: Environmental and Architectural design
Theme: Environments; Imagination

Becky: Case studies 29, 32, 34
Endorsement: Art, Craft and Design
Area of study: Textile Design
Theme: Environments; People

Ben: Case studies 37, 40, 43, 46
Endorsement: Photography
Area of study: Experimental imagery; Photographic installation
Theme: Environments; Objects

Carl: Case studies 28, 31
Endorsement: Three-Dimensional Design
Area of study: Ceramics
Theme: Artists; Objects

Dasal: Case studies 1, 5, 11, 14
Endorsement: Fine Art
Area of study: Painting and drawing
Theme: Environments; Imagination

Esperant: Case studies 17, 20, 26
Endorsement: Graphic Communication
Area of study: Design for print; Illustration
Theme: Imagination; Working from a design brief

Jordan: Case studies 30, 36
Endorsement: Fine Art
Area of study: Painting and drawing
Theme: Faces and portraits

Matthew: Case studies 42, 45, 47
Endorsement: Fine Art
Area of study: Painting and drawing
Theme: Environments; Imagination

Michael: Case studies 2, 7, 12
Endorsement: Three-Dimensional Design
Area of study: Construction; Sculpture
Theme: Animals, birds and insects; Environments; Objects

Nick: Case studies 3, 6, 9
Endorsement: Graphic Communication
Area of study: Design for print
Theme: Working from a design brief

Stuart: Case study 10
Endorsement: Fine Art
Area of study: Painting and drawing
Theme: Artists; Faces and portraits

Yousef: Case studies 19, 22, 25
Endorsement: Photography
Area of study: Documentary photography
Theme: Culture; Environments; Objects

Artists

Dionne Barber: Case studies 16, 21, 24
Endorsement: Fine Art
Area of study: Painting and drawing
Theme: Environments; Objects; People
www.dionnebarber.com

Louise Watson: Case studies 27, 33, 35
Endorsement: Textile Design
Area of study: Constructed textiles
Theme: Environments; Pattern and decoration
www.brunelbroderers.co.uk

Reinhild Beuther: Case studies 4, 8, 13
Endorsement: Photography
Area of study: Photographic installation; Portraiture
Theme: Faces and portraits
www.artnucleus.org

Simon Ryder: Case studies 38, 39, 48
Endorsement: Fine Art
Area of study: Mixed media; New media
Theme: Animals, birds and insects; Imagination
www.artnucleus.org

Glossary

A

10 × 8: a standard size of photographic paper, measured in inches.

Aesthetic qualities: the characteristics or visual aspects of an image or artefact which we regard as beautiful or which provide pleasure to our senses.

Analytical drawing: a drawing that analyses source material in depth.

Analytical studies: studies that analyse source material in depth.

Analytical understanding: seeing and understanding the visual relationships and connections between the elements of an image, composition or design.

Animated sequence: film, animation or motion graphic such as a title sequence for a TV programme or an 'ident' for a TV channel.

Annotations: notes alongside images in your sketchbook, on design sheets or mounts of studies, clarifying ideas, observations or intentions, or making connections clear. This includes acknowledging the source or authorship of contextual material, for example recording the artist, title, date and other detail if you wish, of a work you have made reference to.

Aperture: the hole in a lens through which light passes. The diameter of the aperture can be changed and is calibrated in 'f-numbers' or 'stops'.

Appliqué: literally work laid or applied onto another surface – usually fabrics, lace, etc.

B

Bibliography: a list which documents books, articles, websites, etc. used as sources. It is usually presented in standard form – author, title, publisher, year (if known).

C

Collage: an image made by pasting together assembled fragments of paper or other materials, 'discovered' by Picasso and Braque in the early 20th century.

Collatype: a method of making direct prints by inking up an image made from surface textures or cut or torn cardboard or paper.

Colour: the colours of the spectrum: red, blue, yellow, green, orange, violet, etc.

Colourways: alternative colour combinations – a term used in reference to abstraction, design and pattern, particularly in textiles and printmaking.

Composition: the way in which each part of an image or form relates to each other and to the whole.

Compositional roughs: small studies exploring ways in which the basic shapes or forms of a composition work together in relation to each other, and each in relation to the whole.

Contact prints: small prints made without enlargement for the process of reviewing images in traditional and digital photography.

Content: the lines, shapes, forms, textures and spaces that make the image.

Contextual material: examples of art, craft or design, cultural objects or artefacts, including architecture from different times, periods and cultures.

Continuum: the ways in which the discoveries and advances made in one study or project lead on to the next; seeing your work as part of a whole.

Creative journey: the complete journey of your work from investigation to the development of ideas and the realisation of your intentions.

Critical

Critical response: responding in a structured, well-focused way that shows depth of understanding, informed opinions and ideas, rather than just describing surface appearance.

Critical understanding: seeing and understanding the connections and relationships between images or designs. Also, understanding the ways in which the elements of an image or design relate to each other.

Critical vocabulary: words, including specialist terms, that are used to analyse, compare and contrast works of art, craft and design.

D

Design: the application of aesthetics to functional realisations as seen in graphics, textiles, 3D design.

Design brief: a defined focus for a topic that has specific requirements, for example in Graphic Communication.

Design elements: images, typography, space and layout, line, shape, tone, colour.

Design roughs: small sketches or diagrams exploring how elements of a design or layout work together in relation to each other, and each in relation to the whole. These are often drawn in stylus pen or in fineliner on tracing or layout paper, in pencil on cartridge paper or using electronic media.

Design sheets: sheets on which a sequence of studies show the development of a design or design alternatives.

Designs: images and ideas in Graphic Communication, Textile Design and Three-Dimensional Design.

Digital darkroom: a term often applied to the processing of digital images on a computer using one of the wide range of software programs available.

Digital photography: images that are taken using a digital camera which records information electronically for transfer to a computer or printer.

Documentary realism: images which document an event, usually with human interest and often focusing on a social issue.

Dry brush technique: when a brush loaded with relatively thick paint is gently dragged over the surface of a painting to add a layer of textured colour.

Drypoint: a printmaking method in which a soft metal plate is engraved with a steel point then inked and printed.

E

Electronic media: computer hardware, video and sound recording.

Evaluating: looking back, reflecting on the strengths and weaknesses of an idea or image, comparing ideas and images and making a judgement or decision.

Exposure: the amount of light allowed onto photographic film, an image sensor or photographic paper.

F

Fieldwork: gallery or museum visits, site visits, work done on location.

First-hand sources: source material that you can see and study from direct, first-hand experience. For example, studying a painting in a gallery, working from the landscape or from textured surfaces.

Font: also spelt 'fount'; a set of type of one face or size; in ICT it is commonly used instead of 'typeface' to denote the style of type.

Formal elements: often called visual elements – line, shape, colour, tone, form, mass, volume, space, texture, composition. The language or vocabulary of Art and Design that we use to make images and objects.

Framing edge: the edge of a canvas, board or photograph.

G

Ground: a first layer of transparent paint applied to watercolour paper or illustration board which establishes a ground colour or shade that will affect the appearance of colours applied later on.

H

Hue: a distinct colour of the spectrum; pure colour without the addition of black or white.

I

Image making: creating, forming, constructing, composing, designing, making an image.

J

Journal: a collection of information about technical data, techniques and processes, and reflections on contextual material relevant to the area of study.

Juxtaposed: visual elements such as lines, shapes, colours or objects, images and text positioned in relation to each other.

K

Key colour: a colour that creates a link between other colours used in a painting, e.g. red may provide a key between orange tones and blues/purples.

L

Layout: in graphics, the relationship between design elements such as image, typography, space, as in book covers and magazine pages. Also used when referring to a sheet of multiple images in photography.

Line and wash: there are several versions of this technique using different media and either colour or monochrome. It offers the subtleties of watercolour with the strength and fluidity of line.

Lines of enquiry: the direction you take and your lines of thinking, in investigating sources and ideas, in experimenting with media and in developing your ideas.

Log: a diary, both visual and written that usually relates to an event or experience such as a workshop or gallery visit.

M

Maquettes: small 3D studies or models that explore shape, form and space, often translated from drawings. A maquette is like a 3D working drawing.

Media: plural of 'medium'; the materials of Art and Design activity, e.g. pencil, crayon, chalk, charcoal, clay, plaster, wire, thread.

Monotype: also known as monoprint, a simple method of making direct or indirect prints by drawing directly onto an inked-up plate or drawing on the back of a sheet of paper placed on an inked plate.

N

Negative space: the shapes and spaces between solid forms or positive shapes.

O

Opacity: how dense an image appears – less opacity means that the image appears transparent or see-through.

P

Photomontage: a collection of photographic images combined together in the same scene or frame.

Picture plane: plane of the physical surface of a painting or image.

Posterisation: the process of flattening and separating tonal areas of a photograph.

Process: how you go about something, the process of investigating and developing ideas, the process of research; technical processes such as in printmaking, drawing and painting, in developing a film, or using glazes in ceramics.

Pushing the medium: an expression that refers to experimenting with a medium or technique, pushing it to its limits, finding out what you can do with it.

R

Recording: the process of collecting information in visual, written and other forms and providing evidence of your ideas, observations and insights.

Reflecting: thinking, evaluating, comparing, looking back on progress, considering ideas, your response and directions within the work.

S

Samples: small working studies in textiles, exploring composition and design, texture and colour.

Saturation: depth or intensity of colour.

Secondary sources: source material that you experience through reproductions or images produced by someone else.

Shutter speed: the speed with which the camera's shutter opens, measured in fractions of a second.

Solarisation: the process of reversing tonal areas so that light tones become dark and dark tones become light.

Source material: objects, artefacts or images that you will investigate and develop your ideas from.

Space: an area not filled with solid shapes and forms; relating to the illusion of depth and distance.

Specialist language: the words that are used to define the formal elements of art, craft and design and additional terms that give more detail such as hue, tint, shade, tone, foreground, background, plane, positive and negative shape, translucence, opacity. Each subject area in art, craft and design also has terms that are specific to their media and processes.

Specialist terms: terms that identify the media, techniques and processes of specialisms in art, craft and design.

Starting point: an object, theme, issue or brief.

Subject: the subject of art and design, such as 'landscape', 'the human figure', etc.

T

Techniques: ways in which materials and media can be manipulated to create different visual effects.

Tempera and gouache: opaque water-based media which can provide smooth dense colour by virtue of the quality and amount of pigment used in their manufacture.

Test strips: in traditional photography, test strips using full sheets or strips of photographic paper are used to test exposure times, contrast adjustments and processing time.

Thumbnail drawings, thumbnail sketches, thumbnails: small, rapid, fluent drawings made to quickly make a visual note of an idea, something seen, or of a potential composition.

Tonal contrast: the degree of difference between light and dark tonal values.

Tonal relationships: the ways in which tonal values or degrees of light and shade react with each other to form contrasts and subtleties whether in monochrome (black, white and greys), or in colour.

Translucent: ink or paint which allows some light to pass through it.

Typography: the style and appearance of type for example, in print, an electronic page, a motion graphic, signage system or packaging design.

V

Visual vocabulary: the language of Art and Design; the formal elements that we use to make art, design work or photography.

Visuals: visualisations or 'mock-ups' using a photo-montage technique to show, for example, how an idea for a large sculpture or construction might look in a landscape, a built environment or public space.

W

Wash: a thin layer of water-colour applied with a broad brush or sponge.

Wet on wet: the method often employed in water-colour painting where colour is flooded into a dampened area of paper or where paint is allowed to bleed into an adjacent area of wet paint, creating a soft area of colour with blurred or bleeding edges.

Wet process photography: a process whereby the camera uses a light-sensitive film which is then chemically treated to produce a negative. The image on this is projected through an enlarger in a darkroom onto light-sensitive paper, which is then processed to make the image appear.

Working drawing: a drawing, to scale or full size, that shows the layout, plan, composition for a final piece or study.

Index

Richter, Gerhard **42, 49, 118**
rule of thirds **78**
rust effects **139**
Ryder, Simon **149–50, 152, 180**

S

samples **23**
saturation **94**
scale distortion **153, 163–7, 173, 178**
scraping back **87**
screengrabs **26, 89, 143, 166, 167**
sculptures **15, 25, 47, 48**
scumbling **87**
secondary sources **119, 125**
Seurat, Georges **31**
Shemesh, Lorraine **116**
shutter speed **80, 89, 102**
Simpson, Ian **154–5**
sketchbooks **131–3**
skies **41, 42, 58**
skills, developing **84–6, 134–6**
  critical skills **139–40, 160–1**
  photographic **89, 92, 147**
Small, Andy **153, 163**
solarisation **81**
source material **10, 20, 119**
  collecting **12, 13, 16, 30**
  selecting **61, 63, 64–5**
sources, acknowledging **31**
space **23**
specialist language **31**
specialist terms **56**
starting point **10**
Stewart, Iain **28, 51, 119–20, 121**
stitch, drawing in **129–30**
storyboard **116**
straw constructions **155, 157, 168**
subject **32**
sunsets **11, 42**
surfaces, variety of **123**

T

technical information, photography **27**
techniques **9**
tempera and gouache **69**
test strips **81**
textile artists **129–30**
Textile Design **76–7, 95–9, 111–13, 133, 139**
textile project **60–4**
textiles, Alex's work **61–4, 76–7, 95–9**
textiles, using software **26**
texture **72, 103, 180**
Thoburn, Elliot **29, 69**
three blind mice **69**
Three-Dimensional Design
  Carl's work **114, 126–7**
  developing ideas **16, 24–6**
  recording ideas **114–16, 126**
  resourcing ideas **12**
  realising intentions **168**
  contextual material **46**
  critical response **154**

10 x 8 size **147**
thumbnail drawings **23**
tonal contrast **66**
tonal relationships **32**
tonal values **140**
translucent **129, 136**
Turner, J.M.W. **49, 68**
typeface (font) **179**
typography **21, 179**

U

'undo history' **89**
Uta von Naumburg **15, 26–7, 47**

V

van livery design **9, 34**
viewpoints **83, 93**
visual vocabulary **51**
visuals **24, 178**
Voulkos, Peter **129**

W

Walker, Audrey **129–30**
Warhol, Andy **63**
wash **68, 69**
watercolour methods **68, 72**
Watson, Louise **111, 112–13, 130, 133, 139–40**
wax resist **115, 118, 136**
websites
  Three-Dimensional Design **114**
  architects **154, 155, 168**
  artists **15, 122, 129, 135, 136, 149, 158**
  Barber, Dionne **88**
  embroiderers **130**
  galleries **119, 122, 158**
  Hockney, David **118**

  photographers **119, 153**
  textiles **112**
wet on wet **68, 72, 87**
wet process photography **81, 89**
White, Edwina **70, 85**
work, mounting **178**
working drawing **162**

Y

Yousef's work in photography **80, 81, 82–3, 89–93, 105**